Drupal 7
Multi-sites Configuration

Run multiple websites from a single instance
of Drupal 7

Matt Butcher

[PACKT] open source *

PUBLISHING

community experience distilled

BIRMINGHAM - MUMBAI

Drupal 7 Multi-sites Configuration

First published: March 2012

Production Reference: 1190312

Published by Packt Publishing Ltd.
Livery Place
35 Livery Street
Birmingham B3 2PB, UK.

ISBN 978-1-84951-800-0

www.packtpub.com

Cover Image by Vinayak Chittar (vinayak.chittar@gmail.com)

Credits

Author
Matt Butcher

Reviewers
Surendra Mohan

Veturi JV Subramanyeswari

Acquisition Editor
Sarah Cullington

Lead Technical Editor
Hithesh Uchil

Technical Editors
Vanjeet D'souza

Vrinda Amberkar

Project Coordinator
Yashodhan Dere

Proofreader
Mario Cecere

Indexer
Tejal Daruwale

Production Coordinator
Nilesh R. Mohite

Cover Work
Nilesh R. Mohite

About the Author

Matt Butcher is an Expert Developer at HP Cloud, where he deals with PHP and Drupal development. He is a member of the Emerging Technologies Lab at Loyola University, Chicago, where he is currently finishing a Ph.D. in philosophy.

He has written six other books for Packt Publishing, including *Drupal 7 Module Development* (co-authored with five others), *Drupal 6 JavaScript and jQuery*, *Learning Drupal 6 Module Development*, and *Mastering OpenLDAP*. He has also contributed articles to various websites and scholarly journals. He actively contributes to several Open Source projects.

My sincere thanks to Matt Farina, Greg Dunlap, John Albin Wilkins, Sam Boyer, Ken Rickard, Larry Garfield, and Greg Leroux for fielding various questions during the authoring of this book. Some of the ideas in this book were inspired by Brian Tully, Theresa Suma, and Chachi Kruel at ConsumerSearch.

Thanks to the technical reviewers who made this book better with their thoughtful comments. The team at Packt has been great to work with, and for this book Sarah Cullington and Yashodhan Dere (and their team) have worked tirelessly to bring it to fruition.

And, of course, thanks to Angie, Annabelle, Claire, and Katherine who gave up a portion of our family time to let me write this book. The book's done, kids. We're going to the zoo!

About the Reviewers

Surendra Mohan is a Service Delivery Manager at a well known software consulting European MNC in India.

He completed his BE in 2004 from VTU, Belgaum, in the branch of ISE. He started his career as a Software Engineer with .NET technology. Later he moved into the area of HR/Recruitment/IT Consulting/Software Development/Web Development via Global Solutions while exploring open source web technologies such as Drupal, Ubercart, and so on, handling various roles as a Programmer, Technical Lead, Project Lead, Technical Architect, and other such roles, finally landing as Service Delivery Manager on Drupal.

> I would like to thank the person who introduced me to Packt Publishing for giving me such an excellent opportunity to get associated with them. I would like to thank my family for motivating me and providing me complete support while reviewing this book.

Sree (a.k.a. **Veturi JV Subramanyeswari**) is currently working as Drupal Architect at a well known software consulting MNC in India. Prior to joining this company, she served few Indian MNCs, many start ups, R&D sectors in various roles such as Programmer, Tech Lead, Research Assistant, and so on.

She has around eight years of working experience in web technologies covering media and entertainment, publishing, healthcare, enterprise architecture, manufacturing, public sector, defense communication, gaming, and other such areas.

She has reviewed other technical books such as *Building Powerful and Robust Websites with Drupal 6*, *Learning Drupal 6 Module Development*, *PHP Team Development*, *Drupal 6 Site Blueprints*, *Drupal 6 Attachment Views*, *Drupal E-Commerce with Ubercart 2.x*, *Drupal 7 First Look*, and many more published by Packt Publishing.

I would like to thank my family and friends who supported me in completing my reviews on time with good quality.

www.PacktPub.com

Support files, eBooks, discount offers and more

You might want to visit www.PacktPub.com for support files and downloads related to your book.

Did you know that Packt offers eBook versions of every book published, with PDF and ePub files available? You can upgrade to the eBook version at www.PacktPub.com and as a print book customer, you are entitled to a discount on the eBook copy. Get in touch with us at service@packtpub.com for more details.

At www.PacktPub.com, you can also read a collection of free technical articles, sign up for a range of free newsletters and receive exclusive discounts and offers on Packt books and eBooks.

http://PacktLib.PacktPub.com

Do you need instant solutions to your IT questions? PacktLib is Packt's online digital book library. Here, you can access, read and search across Packt's entire library of books.

Why Subscribe?

- Fully searchable across every book published by Packt
- Copy and paste, print and bookmark content
- On demand and accessible via web browser

Free Access for Packt account holders

If you have an account with Packt at www.PacktPub.com, you can use this to access PacktLib today and view nine entirely free books. Simply use your login credentials for immediate access.

Table of Contents

Preface

Drupal is a flexible Content Management System (CMS). One important feature that it provides is its ability to run multiple websites from one single installation of the Drupal software. This book is about that specific feature. From installation to configuration, then to maintenance and updating, this book focuses on the nuances of what is called "multi-site" Drupal.

The book takes a practical hands-on approach, showing, by example, how to run several sites, each with its own theme, content, and users.

What this book covers

Chapter 1, *Multi-site Drupal*, introduces the broad concept of multi-site, discussing several ways that servers can be configured to run multiple sites. The first half of the chapter focuses on determining which sort of multi-site configuration is best for your needs. The second half focuses on setting up a server environment.

Chapter 2, *Installing Drupal for Multi-site*, covers the process of installing Drupal once, and then configuring several sites to all run on this one Drupal instance. Multi-site configuration can be tricky, but we will methodically walk through the process.

Chapter 3, *Settings, Modules, and Themes*, focuses on adding features to multi-sites. Sometimes features (provided by Drupal modules) are shared across sites, while other times only one of the sites will have a particular feature. We will discuss how this can be achieved. We also look at installing and configuring themes so that each site can have its own distinct look and feel.

Chapter 4, *Updating Multi-site Drupal*, focuses on maintenance tasks. When running multiple sites on a single installation, it can sometimes be tricky to run software updates. This chapter teaches you how to navigate the pitfalls of multi-site configurations in order to keep your site secure, safe, and stable.

Chapter 5, Advanced Multi-sites, covers several advanced topics. We will look at ways to enhance multi-site capabilities, and share limited data between sites. This survey of available add-on modules points multi-site managers to a trove of resources that can take your multi-site to the next level.

What you need for this book

This book assumes basic knowledge of installing and running Drupal. The reader should be comfortable working in a web browser and also have a rudimentary understanding of working from the command line. While this book uses examples from Linux and Mac operating systems, the concepts apply equally well to Windows environments.

Advanced readers will also have the option to work with VirtualBox and Vagrant to quickly experiment with multi-site on its own virtual server running within your normal desktop environment.

Who this book is for

This book is written with the site builder in mind. Those comfortable with running websites and familiar with Drupal will find this book useful. Optional advanced topics will provide experienced site builders with additional tools to broaden their Drupal and web administration knowledge.

As most Drupal installations run on Linux-like operating systems, the examples herein target that environment. However, Windows users will also be able to run the same installation on Windows.

Conventions

In this book, you will find a number of styles of text that distinguish between different kinds of information. Here are some examples of these styles, and an explanation of their meaning.

Code words in text are shown as follows: "And thirdly, the `vagrant up` command tells vagrant to install, boot, and configure our server."

A block of code is set as follows:

```
<VirtualHost *:80>
  ServerAdmin ops@example.com
  DocumentRoot /var/www/
  # Lots more below.
```

Any command-line input or output is written as follows:

```
$ cd sites/books.local
$ mkdir files
$ chown www-data files
$ chmod 755 files
```

New terms and **important words** are shown in bold. Words that you see on the screen, in menus or dialog boxes for example, appear in the text like this: "You can carry out this same step in your web browser by going to http://drupal.org and going to the **Download and Extend** page".

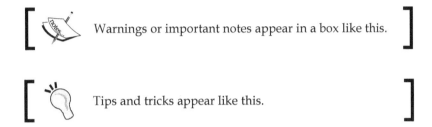

Warnings or important notes appear in a box like this.

Tips and tricks appear like this.

Reader feedback

Feedback from our readers is always welcome. Let us know what you think about this book—what you liked or may have disliked. Reader feedback is important for us to develop titles that you really get the most out of.

To send us general feedback, simply send an e-mail to feedback@packtpub.com, and mention the book title through the subject of your message.

If there is a topic that you have expertise in and you are interested in either writing or contributing to a book, see our author guide on www.packtpub.com/authors.

Customer support

Now that you are the proud owner of a Packt book, we have a number of things to help you to get the most from your purchase.

Use the #PacktDrupalMS hashtag on Twitter to discuss the book with the author, fellow readers, and Packt.

Errata

Although we have taken every care to ensure the accuracy of our content, mistakes do happen. If you find a mistake in one of our books—maybe a mistake in the text or the code—we would be grateful if you would report this to us. By doing so, you can save other readers from frustration and help us improve subsequent versions of this book. If you find any errata, please report them by visiting http://www.packtpub.com/support, selecting your book, clicking on the **errata submission form** link, and entering the details of your errata. Once your errata are verified, your submission will be accepted and the errata will be uploaded to our website, or added to any list of existing errata, under the Errata section of that title.

Piracy

Piracy of copyright material on the Internet is an ongoing problem across all media. At Packt, we take the protection of our copyright and licenses very seriously. If you come across any illegal copies of our works, in any form, on the Internet, please provide us with the location address or website name immediately so that we can pursue a remedy.

Please contact us at copyright@packtpub.com with a link to the suspected pirated material.

We appreciate your help in protecting our authors, and our ability to bring you valuable content.

Questions

You can contact us at questions@packtpub.com if you are having a problem with any aspect of the book, and we will do our best to address it.

1
Multi-site Drupal

In this first chapter we will learn about the basics of multi-site hosting, including what it is and how it works. We will cover the necessary aspects of networking and web serving. The following are the main topics we will cover:

- What multi-site configurations are, and how they differ from standard single-site configurations
- How Drupal's multi-site implementation fits into the picture
- Why and when multi-site configurations are useful
- How domain names and IP addresses are configured for multi-site
- How web servers handle multi-site
- How to configure the Apache server for multi-site
- How to use Vagrant and VirtualBox to quickly build a test environment

By the end of this chapter, we will not only have conceptual knowledge of multi-site configurations, but we'll also have a virtual host configured with Linux, Apache, MySQL, and PHP, and even a shiny new copy of Drupal. This will prepare us for the next chapter, when we dive into Drupal installation.

Drupal is a multi-site Content Management System

Drupal is a web-based **Content Management System (CMS)**. Its purpose is to provide a flexible and powerful system for building a wide variety of websites. To that end, it not only has a flexible content management core, but also provides a modular system in which add-on modules can hook into just about any piece of Drupal. With over seven thousand modules available, Drupal has become a choice tool for constructing robust and feature-rich websites.

It should be evident already that Drupal can do many things. This book is focused on one of those things. A single instance of Drupal can be used to run more than one website. This means you can install the Drupal software once and have it drive more than one website. This feature is called **multi-site hosting**. Over the course of this book, we will learn how to install, configure, and manage a multi-site Drupal instance.

This first chapter covers the basics of running multiple sites. It is conceptually divided into two sections: The first is focused on *what* multi-site hosting is all about, and the second is on how we can start building a multi-site capable server.

In the first part we look at several common ways of building a multi-site—some of which are Drupal-specific, and some of which are not. By the end of this section you will be familiar with the problems that are solved by multi-site installations, as well as what options there are for hosting multiple sites on a single server.

While there are several ways to host multiple sites on the server, this book is focused only on one particular method: Using Drupal's built-in multi-site capabilities to host several sites on one copy of Drupal's code. After reading about other methods, you may discover that one of those suits you better, and where possible I have inserted references detailing those other methods. But for those who see Drupal's multi-site capability as meeting their needs, the remainder of this chapter (and the rest of the book) walks through the process of setting up such a platform.

In the second part of the chapter we will configure a local testing environment. It is not necessary that you run an environment identical to this, but by using Virtual Box and Vagrant to set up a standard virtual machine, this book will create an environment that you should be able to replicate should you so desire. (We will learn more about VirtualBox, as well as manual configuration, later in this chapter.)

To get started, let's look at the relationship between a website and the server that runs it.

From one site to many

In the earliest days of the web it was assumed that each web address (www.example.com) would map to a specific physical server with a specific IP address. This server would be named "www" and its principal purpose would be to serve web pages for a single website. And when the Internet was still relatively young, this was a safe assumption. But the web became far more popular than originally expected, and it experienced explosive growth. One thing that became clear during this period of growth was that it is tremendously useful to be able to run more than one website on a single piece of hardware.

Web servers adapted, adding the capability to map a single IP address of a single server to more than one domain name. So, for example, a single piece of server hardware could handle both `www.example.com` and `www.anotherexample.com`. Many web hosting providers thrived (and still do) by hosting multiple customers' sites on a single physical server.

Over the last decade and a half, server technologies have become more sophisticated. Virtualization of servers, cloud computing, distributing one site over multiple servers, and edge-side caching are just a few of the technologies that have changed the landscape. The initial assumption that one server would host one website has long-since passed away.

Historical reasons have led to the development of multi-site technologies, but for what reasons do people run multi-site installations? And how do you know when you need one?

Why multi-site?

Earlier, I mentioned that multi-site technologies were developed as a response to the needs of system administrators and developers. But what are those reasons? What problems are solved by multi-site configurations? There are many different reasons why people choose to host multiple sites on the same server. Here are several examples:

- Running different software on the same site
- Leveraging shared hosting
- Easing server administration
- Staging and testing a site before it is public
- Sharing a single code base for several sites
- Running secure (HTTPS) and standard (HTTP) sites on the same server
- Building an efficient development environment

Below, we will take a look at each of these examples, understanding what each need is, and how a solution works. But I will state here at the outset that not all of these examples are best addressed with Drupal's multi-site feature.

Running different software on the same site

It is not uncommon to break up a large site into parts and place each part on a separate subdomain. For example, say we have a popular news site located at www.example.com. But this site also has a successful blog. Instead of residing under www.example.com, the blog may be reachable at the separate domain blog.example.com. While this appears to be an isolated site, it may be running on the same hardware. Often, subdomain configurations such as this are done when the two parts of the site run different software. For instance the main site may run on Drupal while the blog site may run on WordPress.

This is not the sort of configuration that Drupal's multi-site feature is built for. Drupal does not natively run other applications. But there are other multi-site configurations (for example, Apache's virtual hosting) that can neatly accomplish this.

Making the most of shared hosting

Sometimes a single operator will run more than one website, and these websites may be completely independent of each other. But to make the most of an existing hosting provider, the operator may choose to run both websites on the same host. This minimizes hosting costs and maintenance hours, but still allows the administrator to host different sites.

I do this, and in my case I have a single account with a web host, and I host multiple sites under that one account. This way I pay one monthly fee regardless of how many sites I operate from that account. And since my sites run Drupal, I take advantage of Drupal's multi-site capabilities.

Easing server administration

Maintaining a server is work. A server requires maintenance and upkeep. And the more servers one maintains, the more effort is required to keep everything running smoothly. For that reason, some choose multi-site configurations just to reduce the amount of maintenance work involved in keeping a server running. It also lowers the cost of server hardware, Internet connectivity, and utilities. But this trade off is not without its drawbacks. When a multi-site server goes down, all of the sites on that server will be inaccessible. (A common way of addressing this hazard is to run at least one other redundant server.)

The main method used for setting up this sort of configuration is called *virtual hosting*, and Apache, Nginx, and other popular web servers support this out of the box. It is a layer higher than Drupal's multi-site feature (though the two can sometimes be used in conjunction).

Staging or testing before deploying to a live site

It is common practice to stage or run quality assurance (QA) testing on server software before pushing it into production. This requires running an identical code base, but on a different set of servers. In an ideal development environment, separate configurations could be stored in such a way that they could be tracked in version control, require little or no configuration when deploying to each of these environments, and pose no security risks.

Drupal's multi-site configuration is often used for this, since staging, QA, and production sites can share the same code base, even with different configuration files. Sites can seamlessly be deployed from one environment to the next.

Sharing a single code base

Taking a step beyond merely easing server administration, even more effort can be saved by sharing not just a server, but the web-serving software as well. Some CMS systems—Drupal is a prime example—can run multiple sites from a single installation of the software. This means that instead of running one instance of Drupal per site, a single download and installation of Drupal can operate several sites. And this eases maintenance and management further: Code only needs to be updated in one place. Modules and themes only need to be placed in one location. In short, it eases not only general system administrative tasks, but also application maintenance tasks.

Running secure and standard (unsecured) tools on the same server

The HTTP protocol on which the web runs is not itself a secure protocol. Data transmitted over plain HTTP is not encrypted or signed. But HTTPS uses the Secure Sockets Layer/Transport Layer Security (SSL/TLS) mechanism to encrypt and sign content. By leveraging multi-site technologies, it is possible to run two sites on the same domain—one accessible over HTTP, and the other accessible over HTTPS. Often, this is done to provide one level of service for "anonymous" traffic and other tools and services for authenticated users.

This level of configuration is tricky, and requires support in the web server software. Typically, Drupal's built-in multi-site tools are not helpful for this kind of configuration, though there are other Drupal add-on modules that can be very handy in this scenario.

Efficient development

So far, the examples have been centered on serving sites to visitors, but there is another problem space that can be addressed with multi-site configuration. This is site development. Site developers may work on more than one site at a time. Sometimes they work on both the released version of a site, and the upcoming next-generation version. Sometimes they work on several different projects, each with its own site. Regardless, it is much easier to have the option of running multiple sites on a development server, or even on a local workstation.

In my own development, I run a local virtual server (Oracle's VirtualBox), which in turn runs Linux, Apache, MySQL, PHP, and three or four different websites at a time. Running all of these sites in one place makes it easy to manage. In fact, the process has become so efficient for me that I sometimes create a separate site (on the same server) just to test out a new feature or two. As this book proceeds, I will discuss several of the tricks I use for keeping this process simple and effective.

As we will see later, there are other ways of using Drupal's multi-site options to provide sophisticated development environments, such as providing each person on a team with their own configuration file, while still keeping all code (including settings files) in a **Version Control System** (**VCS**). This can be a useful way of improving the efficiency of site development when more than one person is working on the same site.

There are other reasons, of course, for running multi-site installations. The examples shown earlier point out some of the situations in which multi-site technologies come in handy. As we've seen, there are multiple ways of implementing a multi-site configuration, and Drupal isn't always the perfect solution for a multi-site challenge.

To get a better idea for which situations are a good fit for Drupal, we need to learn a little more about what are Drupal's multi-site's strong points, and its weaknesses.

Drupal and multi-site

As we have seen, there is more than one way to map multiple sites onto one server. Do we use Apache with virtual hosting? Several virtualized servers on a single physical server? Machine instances in a cloud? Or do we do it with Drupal itself? Each method has its own advantages and limitations.

In this book we are going to focus on just one strategy. We are going to examine how to use Drupal's built-in multi-site support to take one instance of Drupal and serve more than one site. If you are using Drupal for your web CMS, there are some distinct advantages to this method:

- It is probably the easiest configuration to set up and maintain.
- Drupal itself needs to be installed into only one place on your server. This means less data duplication.
- Many Drupal modules can augment Drupal's multi-site handling, giving you advanced capabilities.

The combination of added features and simplified administration is a boon for would-be multi-site administrators. But there are a few drawbacks to using Drupal's multi-site method, and these should be considered before you begin building a multi-site installation.

In fact, there are two limitations that deserve very clear mention:

- **Security**: Since the sites in a multi-site installation share the same code (and the same directory locations), they share the same files. Thus, if a person has access to the server's file system for one site, that person has access to the same files that are used for all of the sites on that multi-site installation. This makes it a less-than-secure fit for cases where different people are managing different sites.
- **Sharing**: While Drupal's multi-sites share the same Drupal source code, they *do not* share the same database data. Nodes, users, and comments in one site are not accessible to the other site. Typically, this is a good thing, but in situations where you *want* sites to share information, this can become a hurdle that multi-site was not designed to clear.

If security between sites is an issue for your configuration — if the different sites are managed by different people — then Drupal's built-in multisite is not the best solution for your needs. Instead, consider using something like Apache's virtual hosting, with each site getting its own distinct Drupal instance. While you will lose the advantages enumerated above, your sites will be protected from mishaps.

On the other hand, if your sites need to access each other's data (or if you really have one site that listens on multiple domains, but serves the same basic content), you may be better off with another Drupal configuration. The powerful Domain Access module for Drupal (`http://drupal.org/project/domain_access`) provides a sophisticated suite of tools for building a single Drupal site that handles different domains. Domain Access is a complex module — a topic worthy of another book this size — so it could not be covered in this book. The best place to start with Domain Access is on the site given above.

It is possible to configure multiple instances of Drupal to share common database tables, but this is not only a complicated setup, but also one with known security and stability issues. This is discussed in more detail in the last chapter.

The sweet spot for Drupal's built-in multi-site support is handling multiple distinct sites (each with its own content, users, and so on) while sharing a single code base. Modules, themes, and even to some extent files can be shared in a multi-site configuration. But nodes, users, and comments are not shared. Later in the book, we will see some ways of sharing a limited amount of data (such as allowing users to log in to all sites using the same username and password). This sharing, however, will not achieve the same level of flexibility that the Drupal Domain Access module provides.

A quick guide to choosing the right multi-site configuration

It is one thing to state the advantages and disadvantages to Drupal's multi-site feature, but another to determine whether or not Drupal is a good fit for your own needs. Here is a quick guide to determining whether Drupal multi-site is the right choice for a given scenario.

Goal	Method(s)
Multiple sites should share the same code, but have separate data	Drupal's multi-site configuration
Multiple sites should share no code or data, but live on the same web server	Virtual hosting with the web server
Multiple sites (or domains) should share the same code and the same data, though they may have different layouts and styles	Drupal with the Domain Access module
Sites should not even share the same operating system or file system, but should run on the same hardware	Virtualized servers or cloud platforms

Again, this is a book about using Drupal's multi-site support and these other three methods are not covered. But Drupal itself can run in any of the environments mentioned above. If you're interested in the other three configurations, you may find it best to start at `http://www.drupal.org/documentation` and read the documentation, or head to `http://groups.drupal.org` and find others with similar needs to your own.

So far we've been focused on what multi-site hosting is about and which configurations are right in which scenarios. But now it's time to narrow the focus and start working on practical matters.

Setting up a server

Now we are ready to move from questions about what a multi-site is to the actual setup and configuration of a multi-site server. Here, we will be creating an environment that, in the next chapter, will run our Drupal-based multi-site.

The first thing we will need is a server. You may choose to use your local computer as a temporary server. Or you may use a server provided by an **Internet Service Provider** (**ISP**). Or you can use a separate dedicated piece of hardware. But for our purposes, we will be creating what is called a **virtual server**—a complete operating system that runs inside of our current operating system. This server will run its own Linux operating system.

As we configure things below, we will be using Apache on Ubuntu Linux. While Apache configurations work essentially the same on all platforms, different operating systems and distributions organize the files in their own ways. You may wish to consult your operating system's documentation to learn about these differences.

 If you are running your sites on a shared-hosting or managed-hosting platform, chances are that you will not need to configure Apache. Instead, you should work with your hosting provider to set up virtual hosting.

In what is left of this chapter, we will focus on creating an environment in which to run our Drupal multi-site. I am going to walk through two ways of doing this:

- First, we can install a virtual machine pre-configured for this book. We do this with the open source VirtualBox and Vagrant tools, along with a custom Drupal Vagrant profile. This route is great for testing things out on your local workstation. It is a great way of building "disposable" sites that we can develop with. They can be created and deleted without impacting your local "host" computer. It's like having your own personal development server(s), but without the hardware cost.

- Second, we can begin with an established server running Apache, MySQL, and PHP. From there, we can just focus on tuning Apache and creating a few MySQL databases. Note, though, that this route will require you to handle getting the rest of the server configured. However, if you are hosting your sites on a managed service provider or shared hosting account, your hosting provider will probably do all of this for you at your request.

In the next section we will look at the VirtualBox and Vagrant method for running a development environment locally. If this is not to your taste, you can skip and move ahead.

Installing a Drupal Virtual Machine with Vagrant

Building a multi-site Drupal installation does not require running Virtual Box and Vagrant. However, I find this sort of virtual machine configuration to be ideal for experimenting with technologies and development environments. And for the sake of this book, using a pre-packaged configuration such as this allows us to quickly setup nearly identical environments.

Drupal.org hosts a project called Drupal Vagrant (`http://drupal.org/project/vagrant`) designed to get you running on a full **LAMP (Linux Apache MySQL PHP)** stack with Drupal in a matter of minutes.

For this book, there is a special version of the Drupal Vagrant project (`http://drupal.org/sandbox/mbutcher/1356522`). It has been tuned and tailored exactly for this book, and you can use it to build an isolated and disposable environment from which you can follow along.

The full instructions for installing this custom version are available at the previous URL, but here is an abbreviated version.

Installing our tailored Vagrant project

The following tools are required to get started:

- **VirtualBox**: This is an open source virtualization environment. It allows you to run "virtual" servers inside of your normal operating system.

  `http://www.virtualbox.org`

- **Vagrant**: This is a tool for managing VirtualBox servers. Because it makes it easy to build complex sites with a command or two, we will be using this.

  `http://vagrantup.com`

- **Git**: Git is a tool for handling revisions of source code or configuration files. Many popular software packages, including Drupal, store code inside of Git repositories.

  `http://git-scm.com/`

You will need to make sure all three of those are installed according to the directions on their respective websites. While this configuration should work on Linux, Mac, and Windows, there have been recent bugs in the Windows 7 version of VirtualBox. Usually, if you stay with the 32-bit version of VirtualBox, things will work fine on Windows as well.

Next you will need to get a copy of the MultiSite Vagrant profile created for this book. The best way to get it is to retrieve it from Drupal.org's Git server (explained here: `http://drupal.org/project/1356522/git-instructions`). If that doesn't work, you can try to retrieve a Git snapshot and work from there (`http://lb.cm/4FJ`).

Now you will need to start configuring things. For simplicity's sake, I am assuming that we are working from a UNIX-like shell. Analogous commands are available in Windows, too.

```
$ cd multisite_vagrant
$ vagrant box add base http://files.vagrantup.com/lucid32.box
$ vagrant up
```

The first line in the code puts us in the right directory to begin. Next, we install a basic Ubuntu Linux server profile. This is used for building virtual servers. And thirdly, the `vagrant up` command tells vagrant to install, boot, and configure our server. It is normal for each of these two Vagrant commands to take a long time.

Once the `vagrant up` command has finished, your host (local computer) will have a virtual machine running with the following:

- A minimal Ubuntu Lucid server
- Apache 2.2
- MySQL 5.1
- PHP 5.3
- Lots of extra tools (such as Xdebug, phpMyAdmin, and xhprof)

Drupal 7, Drush (the Drupal Shell) and a few common modules will also be downloaded, but they are not yet installed. We will talk about these more in the next chapter.

Basic configuration for this book

In addition to the basic installation, the MultiSite Vagrant profile also creates three hostname entries and three databases for you.

In the course of this book, we will be creating three independent sites. These sites will be called **Books.local**, **Cooks.local**, and **Looks.local**. Each will have its own database in MySQL too (`books_local`, `cooks_local`, and `looks_local`). The basic host names and databases have already been set up for you. When you ran `vagrant up`, a script did the necessary configuration in the VM.

But there is still one thing for you to do. You should add the following to your local computer's hosts file (`/etc/hosts` in UNIX-like operating systems):

```
33.33.33.10     books.local looks.local cooks.local
```

This tells your local machine that all of these hostnames can be accessed on your virtual machine.

If you are interested in learning more about the change to the hosts file, it is explained later in the chapter. But as we are focused here on configuring Vagrant we will finish the configuration first.

Connecting to the new Virtual Machine

Now that we have a new virtual machine set up, we can interact with it in several ways.

- **The File System**: When the virtual machine is running, all of the files in the `multisite_vagrant` project are accessible to the virtual machine. That means you can edit them on your host, and have those changes immediately reflected on the virtual server.

- **SSH**: The virtual machine is running SSH. Typing the command `vagrant ssh` will open an SSH connection to your virtual machine, and you can move around on the command line as you would on any Linux box. (Windows users will need PuTTy for this to work. The `http://vagrantup.com/` website has instructions.)

- **Web**: The virtual machine is running Apache. We set up the site to listen on `books.local`, `cooks.local`, and `looks.local`. So pointing your browser to `http://books.local/server-status` should bring up an Apache status page. And the same is true of the other two domains.

So immediately you have three ways to connect to your server. You can also connect to other ports on your virtual server (including MySQL's), but the above cover the common cases.

Finally, before we move on, here are a few Vagrant commands you should know:

- `vagrant halt`: Shutdown the virtual server. You can start its back up with `vagrant up`.

- `vagrant suspend`: Put your virtual host to sleep. This is very useful, and I highly recommend doing this instead of halting. But it does require around a gigabyte of hard disk space.

- `vagrant resume`: Wake your virtual machine up again (after a `vagrant suspend`).

- `vagrant provision`: Re-run the Vagrant build. While it doesn't re-install Linux or reconfigure the core services, it will re-run all of our configuration scripts. With this, we can reconfigure the server without completely rebuilding it from scratch.

- `vagrant destroy`: This will ruthlessly delete your virtual machine. You can then rebuild from scratch using `vagrant up`. It is useful for "do overs".

Vagrant is one option for quickly starting with this book. But since some environments will require manual customization, in the next few sections I will walk through a manual process of configuring hostnames, Apache and MySQL.

If you are running Vagrant you don't need to do these parts. You can skip ahead to the *Summary* section.

Configuring a server (without VirtualBox and Vagrant)

In the previous section we create a virtual server from an existing profile. This made it easy to get an entire server environment configured and running without dealing with the nuances of configuration.

But this is often not an option. Sometimes it is necessary to configure a server manually. This part of the chapter covers manual configuration. Here we walk through the following setup:

- Mapping domain names to IP addresses
- Setting up a webserver (specifically Apache)
- Configuring MySQL

This is a book about building a website, not necessarily about administering a server, so in these sections we will cover only the basic requirements. If you are building production servers, you are encouraged to find other resources more specific to server administration. That said, the following pages should help you prepare a basic server environment.

First, we will look at networking and domain names — a crucial part of our multi-site configuration — then we will move on to web server configuration. By the end of the chapter we will be ready to install Drupal itself.

Domain names and IP addresses

The first thing we need to be able to do is correctly correlate the many sites in a multi-site configuration so that each site is accessible separately. Largely, we are concerned with the process of mapping multiple domain names to a single server. Chances are, if you've ever run a website before you will be familiar at least in part, with the concepts here, but to make sure we're off to a solid start, I will give a very brief explanation of how domain names need to be configured, and how they are related to an IP address. But the process of configuring a TCP/IP stack varies from environment to environment. Here we will only look at configuring host names through a system's **hosts file** — a file resident on the operating system that tells the networking layer how to find certain domain names.

In the TCP/IP networking stack, the function of an IP address is to provide a location identifier for a network interface on a network. When your computer makes a request for a network resource, the request is sent from your computer's networking interface out over the network. Routers, switches, and other pieces of network equipment transport the message over a series of network links until it arrives at the remote networking interface, at which point that computer handles the request. It then returns data through its network interface, and that message is again relayed through the network back to the initial requesting interface on your computer.

One helpful analogy for this process is the physical mail delivery service. A network interface plays (roughly) the role of a mail box. When you drop a letter in the box, it is picked up by the postal service, and channeled through a series of post offices (much like the switches and routers). Finally, it is delivered to the destination post box. And a letter in reply follows that same process back.

Just as a mailbox has a postal address, a network interface on a TCP/IP network has an **IP address**. This is used by the network to determine crucial things about the network interface, such as what network it is on, and where in that network it is located.

A **domain name** is conceptually one level higher. A given IP address can have more than one domain name, just as a large building may have one address, but many businesses occupying it. And when a business moves to a different building, the address will change, but the business name does not. Analogously, the relationship between a domain name and an IP address is not necessarily permanent. The domain can move from one address to another.

But something on the network needs to know how to map a domain name to an IP address. This role is often handled by a series of servers called **Domain Name Service (DNS)** servers. A DNS server is responsible for mapping a subset of the total domain names to IP addresses. There are thousands upon thousands of DNS servers on the Internet. Each is responsible for a certain portion of IP address-to-domain-name mappings. And the DNS system is structured in such a way that when a client requests information on a mapping, it will get an answer even if the authoritative DNS server is on the other side of the planet.

So when you type in a URL in your browser, chances are good that one of the first things your browser does is send the domain name (`www.example.com`) off to a remote DNS server, which will respond with an IP address (10.21.77.101). From there, your computer's networking software will know how to send requests out to that remote host.

IP addresses and domains

It is possible for a single computer to have more than one IP address. And it is possible for a web server, like Apache, to listen for traffic on more than one address. Because of Apache's flexibility, it is possible for Drupal to piggyback on this functionality, and handle sites on multiple IP addresses.

In a multi-site configuration, then, one of the things you will need to handle (regardless of what software you use to host your website) is ensuring that all of the sites on your multi-site have domain names configured. Sometimes this means changing a DNS server on your local network, or requesting that your network admin do this for you. When using a web hosting provider, you can often request that they handle this mapping for you. And sometimes this means requesting a change from your domain name's registrar (the place in charge of handling your domain name registration—places like GoDaddy or Verisign).

Using a hosts file

While the nuances of configuring DNS are beyond the scope of this chapter, we can take a shortcut that will allow us to proceed with our own development.

When building multi-domain sites, you may not need to change any remote DNS servers. You may be able to simply add or modify an entry in your system's **hosts** file. This file contains a set of domain name mappings specific to your computer only. But be warned: when you use this method, it will only impact the computer on which you make the change. Other computers will not have the same mapping.

 Once you are done building and need to make the site public, you will need to configure a DNS server. Contact your network administrator or web service provider to find out how to add your mappings to their DNS services.

In the case where you are running multiple local sites on your computer, you can map these names like this:

```
127.0.0.1    localhost books.local looks.local cooks.local
```

The format of the snippet above is this: The IP address goes first. Your computer always has a self-referential address of `127.0.0.1` (the loopback address). Next come one or more domain names separated by spaces. So the example above says that four domain names (`localhost`, `books.local`, `looks.local`, and `cooks.local`) all reside on this computer. Any traffic to any of these domains should be "looped back" to the computer itself and handled locally.

 If you are following the VirtualBox/Vagrant installation method, we made a similar configuration, but assigned 33.33.33.10 to the hostnames `books.local`, `looks.local`, and `cooks.local` instead of to 127.0.0.1.

The bottom line is this: To use a multi-site configuration with multiple domains, *something* (a DNS server or a host's file) must be able to handle that lookup from each and every domain name you wish to use to an IP address on your server.

Web servers

Once networking is configured, we can move to the next layer and work with the web server. In a nutshell, a web server's responsibility is to listen for network requests that use the HTTP or HTTPS protocols, and then respond to these requests. Sometimes responding is as simple as delivering a static response or sending the contents of a file on the file system. Images are often served like this. Other times the web server may need to coordinate with other software on the system. Other software may generate the response and feed that back to the web server, which then sends the data back to the client. The original **Common Gateway Interface** (**CGI**) worked in this way, and many contemporary web technologies still do. On some servers, like Nginx, PHP is executed this way. Finally, sometimes the web server itself processes and executes code which generates the content. Apache's `mod_php` module executes PHP code in this way. Most web servers, including Apache, Nginx, IIS, and Lighttpd ("lighty") can support the situation where one single computer handles requests for multiple domain names. That is, most web servers can handle multi-site configurations. The exact configuration differs from server to server, so you will need to consult your web server's documentation to learn more. Here we will focus mainly on Apache.

Apache

The Apache server is one of the most popular web servers used on the Internet. Web hosting providers use it. It comes installed on Mac OS X and is readily available on most versions of Unix, as well as on Linux. A special version of it runs on Windows, as well.

 If you are looking to set up a local server environment on Windows, you may wish to look at Acquia's pre-configured Windows/MySQL/PHP/Drupal stack available at `http://acquia.com`.

Apache supports running multiple sites on a single web server through a method called **virtual hosting**. In this system, a single Apache server can act as if it were multiple servers. And it can do this even if there is only one IP address on the system. For example, to handle two sites, we might configure Apache to have two virtual hosts—one for each site. Each virtual host can then have its own configuration file (or its own section in a larger configuration file) tailored to that site's needs. When Apache receives a request, it looks at the HTTP headers to figure out which virtual host should handle the request, and it hands it processes accordingly.

With its long history and devoted development community, Apache has been built to be remarkably flexible. Multi-site configurations in Apache can be quite sophisticated, and many books have been written about building complex services with Apache. But with domain-aware systems like Drupal, Apache's virtual hosting tools aren't even necessary. A much simpler Apache configuration can handle the necessary HTTP details, while Drupal itself can handle the domain mapping.

For a sophisticated site, you may find it most beneficial to configure Apache to take advantage of virtual hosting, but for this book we will err on the side of simplicity and use only a bare-bones Apache configuration.

Configuring Apache for a Drupal Multi-site

In the last section we looked at setting up a local Vagrant-based virtual machine. Now we will turn our attention back to manual configuration. If you are already running Vagrant, this part of the configuration has been done for you (and you can see it in `/etc/apache2/sites-available/books.local.conf` on your virtual machine).

We are not going to walk through the entire process of configuring Apache. Instead, I assume that Apache is already working. We will focus on fine-tuning the existing configuration. We will assume the following about Apache:

- It is installed and configured to listen on port 80.
- It is correctly serving web pages.
- The Apache `mod_rewrite` module is enabled.
- It is correctly executing PHP using `mod_php`.

The first thing we need to do is locate the Apache configuration for the default host. By default, Apache comes with a single host configured. On Ubuntu, which is configured with virtual hosting in mind, the file `/etc/apache2/sites-available/default.conf` contains the default host's configuration. Sometimes this information is in a file called `apache-vhost.conf` or just `httpd.conf`.

 Apache is usually configured to support virtual hosting out of the box. Even though we are creating three sites, we will create only one virtual host (or re-use the default one).

You do not have to edit the default virtual host. If you are comfortable making a new (single) virtual host for our three sites, feel free to do so. The configuration below applies equally to a single default virtual host or a new virtual host.

The default host configuration typically begins like this:

```
<VirtualHost *:80>
  ServerAdmin ops@example.com
  DocumentRoot /var/www/
  # Lots more below.
```

Most of our configuration will happen between the first and third lines above. Take note of the location of the `Document Root`. (You can change it if you want.) We will need to make sure that Drupal is installed at the document root. That is, in the example above, if `/var/www` is the document root, `/var/www/index.php` should point to Drupal's `index.php` file.

Next, after ServerAdmin, insert these two lines:

```
ServerName books.local
ServerAlias books.local cooks.local looks.local
```

These tell Apache that this server is named `books.local` and that it will answer to the names `books.local`, `cooks.local`, and `looks.local`. These are the domains for the three sites we are going to build in this book. Of course, if you were creating the sites `example.com` and `anotherexample.com`, you would enter those hostnames here.

Once this configuration is done, you can restart Apache.

A note on using virtual hosting for each domain

In the previous section we configured Apache without using its built-in virtual hosting to handle each site in the multi-site configuration. We let Apache treat all domains as if they were the same, and in the next chapter we will use Drupal to distinguish sites based on domain names.

If you are running a virtual host for each site, which is a good idea in many circumstances, you will need to do something that may seem counterintuitive. You must point all of your sites to the same document root—the one and only place where Drupal lives. This is done because all sites will use the same installation of Drupal.

In many other respects, you will be able to take advantage of Apache's host-specific configuration. You can still, for example, create separate access logs for each virtual host.

Next we will configure MySQL.

Configuring MySQL

In the previous section we configured Apache. Now we will set up MySQL with three databases—one for each of our sites. Again, if you are using the Vagrant-based virtual host, you will not need to do this part. It has been done already.

Again, we will assume that MySQL is already set up and running, and we will also assume that you can access the MySQL database as a privileged user and create user accounts and databases.

The first thing to do is create three new databases, one for each site. We will call these databases `books_local`, `cooks_local`, and `looks_local` to correspond to our three hostnames.

From a MySQL monitor (such as `mysql` on the command line), issue the following command:

```
CREATE DATABASE books_local;
CREATE DATABASE cooks_local;
CREATE DATABASE looks_local;
```

That is all that is required to create our databases. But we need to explicitly grant permissions for another MySQL user to access these databases. We will configure our Drupal sites to use this account to authenticate to the database. You can create a separate account for each site if you'd like, but we will just create one.

```
GRANT ALL
  ON books_local.*
  TO 'drupal'@'localhost'
  IDENTIFIED BY 'secret';
GRANT ALL
  ON looks_local.*
  TO 'drupal'@'localhost'
  IDENTIFIED BY 'secret';
GRANT ALL
  ON cooks_local.*
  TO 'drupal'@'localhost'
  IDENTIFIED BY 'secret';
```

This will give the user `drupal`, whose password is `secret`, sufficient privileges to access all three of our databases. Notice that the Drupal account has been restricted to connections from the `localhost`. This is designed to prevent a remote user from connecting as our Drupal user.

It is a good idea to test these credentials using another MySQL client. This will help us preemptively troubleshoot. Here is an example from a UNIX shell using the `mysql` client.

```
$ mysql -u drupal -p secret books_local
mysql> SHOW TABLES;
Empty set (0.00 sec)
```

The snippet above shows that we connected to the database with our credentials, then successfully executed the SHOW TABLES SQL statement.

At this point, MySQL should be ready for Drupal, and we are done preparing the environment.

Summary

In this chapter we explored the basics of multi-site configurations. Then we turned toward practical matters and walked first through the configuration of a Vagrant-based virtual machine for local testing, and then through the manual steps of configuring Apache and MySQL.

In the next chapter we will turn our full attention to Drupal, where we will install our three sites.

2
Installing Drupal for Multi-site

In the previous chapter we set up a server environment for running Drupal. In this chapter, we are going to install Drupal and create three different sites. We will cover:

- Downloading and installing the code
- Creating a default site
- Adding two additional sites

While we are setting up three sites, there is nothing special about that number. A multi-site can have two or more sites.

Manual setup

When preparing our environment for setting up a Drupal multi-site, we first walked through a setup using a special Vagrant virtual machine profile. Then we looked at the manual configurations necessary for Apache and for MySQL. Specifically, we set up an Apache virtual host capable of listening for all three of our hosts (`books.local`, `cooks.local`, and `looks.local`). Then we created three databases in MySQL: `books_local`, `cooks_local`, and `looks_local`.

It is best to create one database per site. Only when absolutely necessary should you install multiple Drupal sites into the same database instance. For example, if you are only allocated a single database instance for multiple sites, you can use Drupal's database prefix feature, which is documented online at `http://drupal.org/documentation`.

Running the custom Vagrant profile gives us not only a complete Linux/Apache/MySQL/PHP stack, but also pre-configures the environment for Drupal. And since Vagrant runs its own virtual server, all of this is done without changing the host system. Not only does Vagrant set up the requisite databases, but it also automates the process of downloading the latest version of Drupal 7 (Vagrant downloads, but does not install).

For a manual installation, though, this is something we will need to do on our own. We will walk through this process in this section. Vagrant users can skim or skip ahead to the *The web installer* section.

Downloading Drupal

In this section we are going to download Drupal and put it in the correct location on the file system. Again, if you have installed the Vagrant profile, this step is unnecessary. This is because the profile already downloaded and unpacked the most recent version of Drupal 7. Here we will see the manual version of the process Vagrant does automatically.

Other Operating Systems

In the last chapter we focused on a Linux setup, but at this point it does not matter which operating system is running. While the commands shown here are on a UNIX shell, the same process is applicable to Windows and OS X. If you are using a database other than a MySQL-like database, you should consult Drupal's documentation to make sure there are no configuration nuances particular to that database.

Drupal is available for download from `http://drupal.org/project/drupal`. At the time of this writing, Drupal 7.12 is the current release. We will download it and move the contents to the web server's document root (`/var/www` in the configuration we created earlier). Following is how it is done in a UNIX shell:

```
$ cd /tmp
$ wget http://ftp.drupal.org/files/projects/drupal-7.12.tar.gz
$ tar -zxf drupal-7.12.tar.gz
$ mv /drupal-7.12 /var/www
```

The command fetches a recent copy of Drupal using the `wget` command-line HTTP client. You can carry out this same step in your web browser by going to `http://drupal.org` and going to the **Download and Extend** page. Next, we uncompress and unpack the archive in one step. Then we move the contents of the archive to the document root we configured earlier. Recall that in the last section, when we configured Apache we declared that the server's document root (`DocumentRoot`) was `/var/www`. That is where our Drupal files must go.

> **The Vagrant profile's document root**
>
> In the Vagrant profile, the document root is in `/vagrant/public/drupal/www`, which is available on both the host computer and the virtual machine. Drupal is installed there.

Once you are done, double check to make sure that `/var/www/.htaccess` and `/var/www/index.php` exist. While those are not the only two files in the directory, they are both very important. If they are missing, something in those four steps has gone awry.

We have three databases ready and Drupal is now located in the correct place, but it is not technically *installed*. To install Drupal, we will need to perform a pair of minor tasks on the command line (or through a graphical file manager) and then run Drupal's web-based installer.

Installing the first host

With the Drupal source code in the document root and the databases created in MySQL, we are ready to install our first site. There are two parts to installing Drupal. The first is done through the operating system, and involves creating a few directories and a file.

If you are manually installing, you will need to copy the settings file and then create a files directory with the correct permissions.

If you are using the Vagrant installation discussed in the last chapter then you do not need to do either of these things. Vagrant does them for you.

Telling Drupal about our sites

Drupal stores most of its data inside of the database. But some things can (or must) be stored in a file on the filesystem. For example, information about connecting to the database must be stored in a file.

Here is where things get interesting for a multi-site installation. Each of our sites will share the same copy of Drupal. But they will not share the same database. Each will have its own. In fact, sites will not share configuration files at all. Each site must have its own configuration files. Sites also will not share many other assets, including uploaded files and certain generated data.

> In cases where a database prefix is used, multi-site works by creating separate sets of database tables for each site. This is complicated and has both security and stability implications. Consequently, it should only be done when no other option is available.

So we have two questions to answer: First, how do we tell Drupal what sites we want to run? Second, how do we pass Drupal site-specific configuration data?

The answer to the first is that we create special directories for each site. And the answer to the second is that we create a settings file in each directory.

Creating a site folder

The most sophisticated element of Drupal's multi-site configuration is also its most mundane. Telling Drupal about the sites we want to host is a matter of creating directories. But a lot of information can be encoded in this folder's name. To understand this, let's take a look at Drupal's default configuration.

Inside of the Drupal code, there is a directory called sites/. If you have done any administration work on Drupal before, this is a directory with which you will be familiar, for all non-core code goes somewhere beneath this directory. In the generic Drupal installation there are two directories inside of sites/. The first, all/ is commonly considered to be the place where downloaded themes and modules go. The second, default/, is commonly considered the place for configuration and for custom modules and themes. While these assumptions hold for a generic single-host site, they don't necessarily mean the same thing for a multi-site.

The all/ directory is the location for information shared across all sites. We will come back to this and treat it in detail in the next chapter.

The default/ directory is the location Drupal looks for, for site configuration information if no other site configurations are found. In that way, it is the *default site*. You can place settings, modules, themes, and files all in subdirectories in this folder, and they will be considered to be part of the default site.

But here's the big tip for building multi-site Drupal: You can create other directories inside of `sites/`, and Drupal will assign these directories special meaning. More specifically, besides `all/` and `default/`, Drupal will assume that all other directories represent a hostname or a hostname pattern.

Domain name directories

Here is an example of domain name directories. If we created a directory called `sites/www.example.com/`, Drupal would assume that we were describing a domain called `www.example.com`. When a request for `http://www.example.com` comes into Drupal and the above directory exists, Drupal will assume that it should answer the request using the configuration files found in the `sites/www.example.com/` directory. But if that server got a request for `http://www.anotherexample.com` or even `http://example.com`, it would answer that request from the configuration in `sites/default/`, for neither of those domains match `sites/www.example.com/`.

What if we wanted to declare a host that answered to both `www.example.com` and `example.com`? Here, Drupal packs another surprise. It treats a directory as a domain name *part*, not necessarily a complete domain name. So if we were to create a directory called `sites/example.com/`, it would be used for both `http://example.com` and `http://www.example.com`. And it could also be used for any other request for a hostname that ends in `example.com`, including `web.example.com` and `another.www.example.com`.

Drupal always searches with respect to specificity. The more specific match always matches over the more general. So say we have the directories `sites/www.example.com/`, `sites/example.com/`, and `sites/com/`. (`sites/com/` is a valid site entry in Drupal.) A request for `www.example.com` would always go to the site described in the `sites/www.example.com/` folder because that is the most specific match.

Keep in mind, as you create these domains, that Drupal will only ever answer domains on requests that Apache passes through. That is, Apache has to be configured to handle these domains before Drupal will even get a chance to handle requests on that domain. We configured Apache for this in the last chapter. By combining Apache host configurations and Drupal sites directories, you can build sophisticated domain mappings without worrying about bogus mappings.

Domains with subdirectories

Our sites are built on the mapping in the previous section—host names to folders—but Drupal can even provide one more layer of matching.

In some circumstances, instead of splitting sites by domain name, you may wish to host them on the same domains, but in different URI paths. That is, you may want `http://www.example.com/site1` to be one site, and `http://www.example.com/site2` to be another site. Drupal supports this configuration as well. But in a way that might be a little confusing.

You won't create a `sites/www.example.com/` folder and then `site1/` and `site2/` folders. Instead, you will convert the slashes in the URL into dots, and create a single directory for each site: `sites/www.example.com.site1/` and `sites/www.example.com.site2/`. As Drupal performs its site search, it will do a similar conversion of directory names to dotted folder names. And again the same specificity rules apply: If a site directory called `www.example.com` also exists, a request for `http://www.example.com/site1` will match the `sites/www.example.com.site1` directory because it is the most specific.

The sites.php special configuration file

Finally, there is one more way to map hostnames to directories. Drupal 7 supports a special mapping file, `sites/sites.php`. In this file you can declare an array of mappings from site names to site folders. For example, say we have an old domain name, `paperbacks.local`, which we want to map onto the `books.local` site. We can do this by creating the `sites.php` file in the `sites/` directory and adding this:

```php
<?php
sites['paperbacks.local'] = 'books.local';
```

This will effectively answer all traffic on `paperbacks.local` as if it were traffic from the `books.local` site. While this technique can occasionally come in handy (especially for development servers), many times you are better off using a redirect in Apache's configuration files rather than serving the same content through two domains.

This is a lot of information to digest, but here are the most important points to remember:

- The `sites/` folder in Drupal is where Drupal looks for site-specific configurations
- Directories (besides `all/` and `default/`) should be named to match host names

- When there are multiple directory names that might match a requested hostname, Drupal will choose the most specific one

If you are in the thick of configuration and need a refresher on this information, check out the `sites/default/default.settings.php` file, which has a summary of this information.

Considering all of this, it is time to create our first site folder. And here we have some options.

How do we decide which to choose?

We are creating three sites in total: `books.local`, `cooks.local`, and `looks.local`. So when creating our first site, we could choose from at least three different options:

- We could use the `sites/default/` directory as the main one for our `books.local` site. This will make `books.local` a truly default site.

- We could create a `sites/local/` directory, which we will assume maps to `books.local`, but which will also map to any other hostnames that end with `.local`. Since we would later create more specific directories for `sites/cooks.local` and `sites/looks.local`, creating things this way would not stop us from achieving our goal.

- Finally, we could just create `sites/books.local/`, which would be specific to our site.

How do we decide which to do? First, none of these is wrong. Each may have its uses in a given situation. But sometimes one solution is better than the others.

On a production site, it is often best to have *something* configured in the default site (`sites/default/`). Sometimes this may be a permanently disabled site. Sometimes it really will be the site that should be treated as the default. But it is best to take measures to prevent the possibility of someone reaching the default site and finding a Drupal installer ready for installation.

 In the Vagrant profile Apache is configured to only direct specific domains to Drupal. As long as those domains have site directories, there is no chance of the default site being run.

On a development site, specificity may be preferable. (The Vagrant version has been configured thus.) You may not want a default instance because you may want to keep all of your sites in their own subfolders for ease of use. It is much easier to find a site's configuration when it has a fully named directory. The innocuous `sites/default/` folder can become an accidental hiding place.

Again, though, there are no wrong answers here. Just make sure you keep security in mind. As we continue, we will use `sites/books.local/` for the reason I mentioned above: This is more explicit and easier for us to find. While this folder already exists in the Vagrant file, to create it manually we will just need to execute a few commands. Starting from the document root, we only need to do this:

```
$ cd sites/
$ mkdir books.local
```

That will create our new `books.local/` directory inside of the `sites/` directory. The next step is to create a few necessary files inside of this directory.

Settings

All of the site-specific content for our `books.local` site is going to go inside of the `sites/books.local/` directory we just created. And the first thing to place in this directory is the settings file.

If you are familiar with Drupal already, you have probably worked with the `settings.php` file. This is the file that holds the database configuration, many PHP configuration directives, and occasionally Drupal variables that need to be accessed very early in the bootstrapping process. Each of the sites in our multi-site configuration must have its own `settings.php` file. And the best way to get started on this is to simply copy the default settings file. Assuming you are already in the `sites/` directory, here is the UNIX command you would run to copy the file:

```
$ cp default/default.settings.php books.local/settings.php
$ chmod 777 books.local/settings.php
```

The first command copies the default file into the `books.local/` directory. Note that the name of this file must be `settings.php`. The second command sets the mode (file permissions) on the file to `777`, which effectively grants any UNIX user read, write, and execute permissions on the file. Normally, this is a dangerous mode to assign to a file, but we do this here just long enough to allow the installer to run. The installer must be able to read and write the file. It will then try to lock down the file for us by changing its mode to something appropriately restrictive.

 If you are using the Vagrant profile, this has been done for you already by the Vagrant installation scripts.

Finally, if you wish, you can edit the `settings.php` file, setting the appropriate database connection details. This will save you some time in the web installer. However, if you prefer to configure this through the web interface, you may do so.

Here is an example configuration section that connects to the `books_local` database we created in the last chapter. If you are using the Vagrant profile, this has already been generated for you, and you can look at the file in `vagrant/public/drupal/www/sites/books.local/settings.php`.

```
$databases['default']['default'] = array(
  'driver' => 'mysql',
  'database' => 'books_local',
  'username' => 'drupal',
  'password' => 'secret',
  'host' => 'localhost',
);
```

The code tells Drupal that the default database for this host is `books_local`, with the user `drupal` and the password `secret`. Finally, it tells Drupal to connect to the database on the `localhost`. If your database server were on a remote host, you would put that host name here instead.

 The `settings.php` file is actually a PHP source code file. But in spite of the fact that all PHP coding constructs can be used here, only configuration directives should be used.

While the database section of the configuration file can be set up to serve more sophisticated purposes (such as connecting to multiple database servers), we are concerned with multi-site right now. So we will forgo a full discussion of database configuration. The INSTALL files that come in the Drupal source code explain many of the other database configuration options.

At this point our settings file is ready, and we can proceed.

The files/ folder

We have only one more thing to do before running the web installer. We need to create a directory where Drupal will be able to write content. Certain data such as file uploads, image thumbnails, and aggregated CSS and JavaScript files need to be stored on the filesystem instead of within the database. So Drupal will need a directory into which it can write these files. Traditionally, this is the `files/` directory (though you can rename it if you want to go through the extra configuration hassle). By default, Drupal will look inside of a site directory for a subdirectory named `files/`. In a default Drupal instance, then, this would be in `sites/default/files/`.

Older versions of Drupal stored the `files/` directory directly in Drupal's root directory. That sometimes caused confusion with multi-site configurations.

Again, with a multi-site configuration, we need each site to have its own `files/` directory. We will create `files/` in `sites/books.local/`. In addition to creating the directory, we need to set permissions on this directory so that Drupal can write to it. In UNIX, the web server (which runs Drupal) runs as a particular user. That user will need to be able to write into `sites/books.local/files/`.

 If you are running PHP as a CGI or as a FastCGI, consult the documentation to discover which user runs those processes. That is the user that will need to own the files directory.

The safest way to configure the `files/` directory permissions is to modify the directory's owner to be the web server user, and then give that user write access. In the following example, the web server is running as `www-data` (the username used on Debian and Ubuntu Linux. Other common user names are `apache`, `http`, and the special UNIX user `nobody`.)

```
$ cd sites/books.local
$ mkdir files
$ chown www-data files
$ chmod 755 files
```

The four preceding commands, do the following:

1. Make sure we are in the right directory.
2. Next, create the `files/` directory.
3. The `chown` (change owner) command sets the owner to the web server's `www-data` user.
4. And finally the `chmod` command changes the mode to `755`, which allows the owner all permissions (7), while giving others only read and execute access (5).

The files in the `files/` directory are treated as public files (files that are generally accessible). Drupal 7 also adds support for private files directories. Private files directories are stored outside of the web server root, and can have any name necessary. If you need to create private files directories, consult Drupal's documentation. The process is no different for multi-sites than for single-site installations.

With our files directory configured, we are ready to move on to the web-based installation.

The web installer

We have configured the base directory for our `books.local` site and created a `settings.php` and a `files/` directory. And in the last chapter we configured Apache to handle directing requests for `books.local` to our Drupal multi-site instance. So we should now be able to run the Drupal web installer.

> **Vagrant does not run the web installer**
>
> To this point, our entire manual configuration has been handled in the Vagrant profile. But this step is not done automatically. So regardless of whether you have been following a manual process or using the Vagrant profile, you will need to run the Drupal web installer.

Just as with a normal installation of Drupal, the installer can be run at `http://books.local/install.php`. We will very quickly walk through the installer.

On the first screen, we are asked to select either a standard or minimal installation. Neither choice will impact multi-site configuration, so we will go with the default, **Standard**.

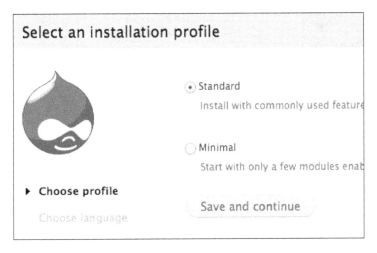

Clicking **Save and continue** will bring up the next installer screen, which allows us to choose a language bundle. By default, Drupal only comes with English, and we will leave that default selected, hitting **Save and continue** to proceed.

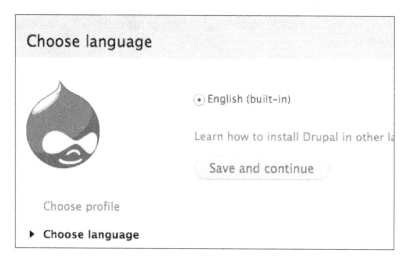

The next stage of the installation is typically the database configuration screen. However, in the previous section we already set our database parameters, so that step will be skipped automatically, forwarding us to the big step—the installation process.

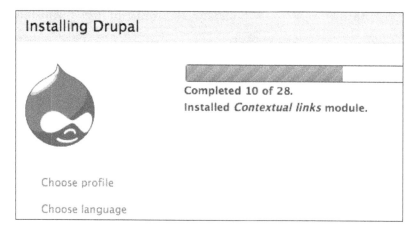

The installer will sequentially install Drupal's core and then the module files. Largely, this is a matter of creating tables in the database and then inserting necessary content, such as settings and defaults.

Once this is done, we are presented with a final installation step—adding site information.

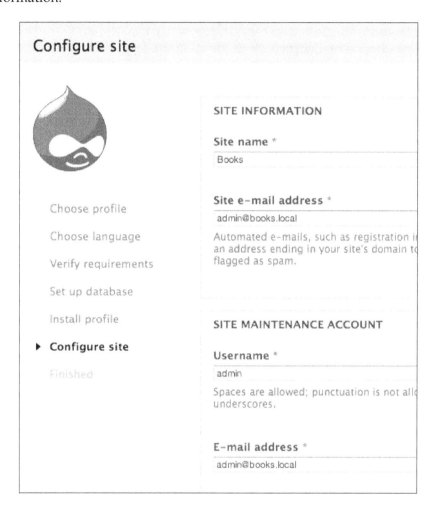

This lengthy form is for adding necessary information about the site, including the site's name and an e-mail address for notifications, information about the administrative user, and default information about site settings such as time zone information.

The user you create here is a special user. It will have unrestricted access to Drupal data, along with maximal permissions. Like UNIX's root user, this first user will be very powerful. For that reason, it is recommended that this user not be associated with an individual, but be given a generic name like "admin." The account can then be used for administrative tasks, but not daily use by the CMS.

When setting up a multi-site Drupal installation, it is allowable to direct the administration e-mail from all sites to the same e-mail address. However, there is a trick that facilitates this and will make your life easier: Many e-mail servers will allow you to insert a tag into your e-mail address that can be used to sort mail on your mail reading client. For example, if my administrative e-mail account is `admin@example.com`, I can add this tag in by adding a plus sign (+) after the name portion of my address, and then putting the tag between the plus sign and the at-sign (@): `admin+books@example.com`. Drupal allows this syntax. On your mail client, then, you can set up filters to sort, flag, or otherwise process e-mail by tag.

Once this form is filled out and submitted, Drupal should display a success message, like this:

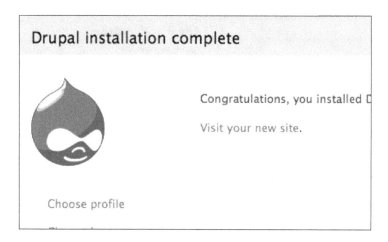

Clicking on **Visit your new site** will take us to the default home page of the newly installed `books.local` site.

Note that we will be automatically logged in as the user we created above, which allows us to begin the task of setting up and configuring our site. But instead of continuing configuration of `books.local`, we will move on to create our other two sites.

Creating the other sites

We spent a long time walking through the process of creating the `books.local` site. The good news is that the process for creating the other sites is the same. Rather than repeating the process in detail, we will look at the process again in summary form, this time doing two sites at once.

Recall that our remaining sites are cooks.local and looks.local, and that we have already created the databases cooks_local and looks_local, one for each site.

Let's begin, in the Drupal sites/ directory, we need to create two directories, cooks.local and looks.local.

Each directory needs a settings.php file. The easiest way to proceed is to copy the settings.php from books.local and change the database information:

```
$databases['default']['default'] = array(
   'driver' => 'mysql',
   'database' => 'cooks_local',
   'username' => 'drupal',
   'password' => 'secret',
   'host' => 'localhost',
);
```

The lines that typically need changing are highlighted above. And these will need to be set in each site's settings.php file.

Remember that these settings files must be writable by the web server. Also, each of the sites directories must have a files/ directory with permissions set so that the web server can write to these directories.

In turn, each site's web-based installer must be run. The installers will be available on http://cooks.local/install.php and http://looks.local/install.php.

At the end of this installation process, we have three different sites installed. While they share a codebase, they have different database backends. This means that each site can have content isolated from the others.

That is all there is to creating a multi-site Drupal installation. While some additional care needs to be taken while setting things up, the installation process is not necessarily harder.

Getting installation help

Sometimes installations fail. This can happen for a variety of reasons. Sometimes the environment does not fulfill one of Drupal's requirements. Sometimes there is a permissions problem either on the file system or the databases. And sometimes bugs in code turn up. This can be a frustrating experience. Where do you turn for help?

Following are the best resources for trouble shooting a Drupal installation, in order:

- **The README.txt and INSTALL.txt documents**: These come packaged with Drupal, and provide a surprising amount of information that will help troubleshoot installation issues. There are even database-specific installation documents (INSTALL.mysql.txt, INSTALL.pgsql.txt, and so on) with information tailored to your selected database environment.

- **The online Drupal installation manual**: http://drupal.org/ documentation/install. This covers the installation process in depth, with many extra notes for exceptional circumstances.

- **Community support**: Available in the form of Drupal Groups (http://groups.drupal.org) and Drupal's IRC (#drupal on Freenode.net). Drupal Groups are forum-based, while the IRC rooms are a great way to connect with people and chat.

- **Local community meet-ups**: Through Drupal Groups (http://groups. drupal.org) you may be able to find a local Drupal Users Group or similar meet-up. These groups often provide a great venue for getting informal support.

These resources will help you through installation difficulties. Drupal has a vast user base with hundreds of thousands of successful installations. It is unlikely that you will come away from these resources with an unanswered question about installing Drupal.

Summary

This chapter focused on installing Drupal. We spent most of the time looking at the first site, paying attention to the details as we walked through the process of installing the books.local site. From there, we installed the other two sites in rapid succession, and by the end of the chapter we had three sites running on a single copy of Drupal's code.

In the next chapter we will work with Drupal's module and theme systems, seeing how a multi-site installation works with these.

3
Settings, Modules, and Themes

In the previous chapter we installed three sites into our one Drupal multi-site, but we did not configure any of these three. In this chapter we will look at configuring Drupal, with a special focus on using Drupal modules and themes. In particular, we will see how Drupal can share modules and themes when we want, but also keep certain modules and themes restricted only to a specific site. We will cover the following:

- Configuring each site separately
- Sharing configurations
- Installing shared modules
- Installing unshared (single-site) modules
- Installing themes and subthemes

Configuring sites

We wrapped up the last chapter by running the Drupal web installer for all three sites, giving each its own database, site name, and configuration. In this chapter we will pick up where we left off.

The important thing to be aware of, given our multi-site configuration, is that each site will have completely distinct settings.

In Drupal, there are typically two places where settings information is stored. The first is in the `settings.php` file, and as we saw from the previous chapter, each site has its own.

The second place is in the database. Settings are stored in the database table named `variables`. This general table stores a wide variety of information in key/value pairs. Again, as we saw in the previous chapter, each site has its own database.

By default, there is no shared location in which configuration common to all sites can be stored. This means that if you have an assortment of configuration data that you want to share across sites, you have two options:

- **Duplicate the data**: You can set the same information for each site
- **Create a shared settings file**: You can add a little logic to each settings file that will direct each Drupal instance to load a shared settings file

 There are ways to share database tables, but this is a very dangerous practice, and is discouraged by Drupal developers. It would be particularly bad practice to attempt to share the `variables` table. In the final chapter, we will see some alternatives for efficiently and securely sharing content across sites.

Let's take a quick look at how we can share settings using settings files.

Creating a shared configuration file

Most of the time it is best to keep site configuration separate for each site. But with tightly related sites, it is sometimes most expedient to share some configuration. The best example of this is when a staging and a production site run on the same server.

Let's say we want to set the site slogan to be the same for all three sites. We want it to say "Quality Information".

Normally, we would set this information through the administrative interface by going to **Administration | Configuration | Site** information and entering our site slogan in the **Slogan** field. But we could also hard-code a slogan by adding the following line to the end of the `settings.php` file:

```
$conf['site_slogan'] = "Quality Information";
```

By setting this for the **Books** site, we will see it displayed on the front page:

Once we have hard-coded this value in the settings file, it cannot be overridden through the administrative interface. For this reason, putting settings in the `settings.php` files should only be used when absolutely necessary.

Our goal, in this trivial example, is to set the site slogan so that it is always the same on all three sites. And we want to create a shared configuration file to do so. This will require adding a little logic to the end of all three of our `settings.php` files.

```
if (file_exists('sites/all/shared-settings.php')) {
  include 'sites/all/shared-settings.php';
}
```

Now the settings files will each try to load the file `sites/all/shared-settings.php`. As a safety precaution, we first check to see if the file exists before loading it. That way, a missing file doesn't cause the entire site (or, in this case, all three sites) to fail.

Now we can create this shared settings file in `sites/all/shared-settings.php`. Here is what the file looks like:

```
<?php
  /**
   * @file
   * Shared settings for all multi-sites.
   */
  global $conf;

  $conf['site_slogan'] = "Quality Information";
```

There are four things to note about this file:

- First, like `settings.php`, we need to explicitly include the `<?php` at the beginning so that the PHP interpreter is switched on.

- Second, we begin the file with a Drupal-standard documentation block. This is just good form, making it easy for others to see what this file is here for. It can also be parsed by the Drupal documentation generator (or by Doxygen, the tool upon which it is based).

- The third thing to notice is this very important line:

  ```
  global $conf;
  ```

  Without it, our attempts to share configuration will silently fail. This tells PHP to share the same `$conf` variable that the site's `settings.php` file is using. Drupal is smart enough to know that for the Books site, this shares the `books.local/settings.php`, and for the Looks site, it should share the `$conf` variable with `looks.local/settings.php` and so on. (This is a simple vestige of the fact that the settings file loads the shared settings file. There's nothing magical about the association.)

- Finally, the fourth thing is the configuration directive itself. As you will have noticed, this is exactly the same as the one I showed earlier. We've just moved it from `settings.php` to `shared-settings.php`.

  ```
  $conf['site_slogan'] = "Quality Information";
  ```

But this time, the `site_slogan` will be added to the configuration of each of our three sites. So now we will see **Quality Information** not just on the Books site, but also on the other two. For example, here is the Looks site using the previous configuration:

So with a few extra lines at the bottom of each settings file, we can create a shared space for declaring settings.

A word of warning about sharing settings

Sharing settings can be a great idea when it comes to simple information, like labels and slogans, and even themes. But there are certain configurations that should typically not be shared, like primary databases, caches, and hash keys. Sharing these can have odd side effects, like the data from one site showing up in another unexpectedly.

Also, keep in mind that the only thing that is actually shared through this mechanism is the data in the settings file. For example, we could tell all three sites to use the same maintenance theme by adding this line to the shared settings file:

```
$conf['maintenance_theme'] = 'bartik'
```

But each site may still configure the Bartik theme differently. Only the one value—which theme to use as the administrative theme—is set in the shared configuration. The rest of Bartik's configuration information is left site-specific.

With these caveats in mind, though, we can share settings across sites.

Let's continue on by looking at modules.

Configuring modules

If you have worked on Drupal before, you have likely heard the following advice given about where you should put your modules:

- Modules that are downloaded from Drupal.org (or elsewhere) should be stored in `sites/all/modules/`
- Modules that you have created should go in `sites/default/modules/`

 The fact that this is a common suggestion does not mean it is the only suggested method, or even the best. There are several competing conventions for how you should organize modules. Each has its advantages and disadvantages.

This advice is convenient for situations in which there is only one site. But for multi-site configurations, things get more complicated.

The `sites/all/` directory houses data that is shared among all of your sites. The `sites/default/` directory houses data used only for the default site (and in our current configuration, we're not using this directory). And the `sites/SITENAME/` folders (`sites/books.local/`, `sites/cooks.local/`, and `sites/looks.local/`) contain data specific to the named site.

This all has very practical implications for our sites:

- If a module is stored in `sites/all/modules/`, then all of our sites will have access to the module

- If a module is stored in `sites/books.local/modules/`, then only the Books site will have access to that module

- If a module is stored in `sites/default/modules/` (and we have no default site), then no sites will be able to access the module

The same goes for themes and `theme/` directories. It should be clear, then, that at least some of the more conventional methods for structuring module directories simply do not apply well to a multi-site configuration.

Another common pattern that works better is to store your custom modules in a subdirectory called `custom/`. This directory can be stored in `sites/all/modules/custom/` or `sites/SITENAME/modules/custom/` or both. Likewise, modules from Drupal.org are stored in `contrib/` directories. The Vagrant profile automatically creates and utilizes a `contrib/` directory for add-on modules.

Let's take a look at how this works out.

Sharing modules

The **Media** module is a popular module for managing media such as images, videos, and audio files. Information about this module can be found at `http://drupal.org/project/media`. Let's install this module as a shared module—one that can be used by all of our sites.

The first thing to do is to get the module. You can download it from the URL and then uncompress the file and place its contents in `sites/all/modules/contrib/`. If you are using the Vagrant profile or have installed Drush (the Drupal Shell), you can run this command from the top level of your Drupal installation (the directory that has `index.php` and the `sites/` directory in it).

```
$ drush dl media
```

Vagrant users should run `vagrant ssh` to connect to the VM and then run the command from within the VM's `/vagrant/public/drupal/www` directory.

Once this command has run, you should be able to find the directory `sites/all/modules/contrib/media/`.

Logging in as the administrator on the Books site, we can check for this module in **Administration | Modules**:

▾ MEDIA		
ENABLED	NAME	VERSION
☐	File entity	7.x-1.0-rc2
☐	Media	7.x-1.0-rc2
☐	Media Internet Sources	7.x-1.0-rc2

All three of these modules—**File entity**, **Media**, and **Media Internet Sources**—come with the Media module. Let's enable all three by checking the box and then pressing the **Save Configuration** button at the bottom of the screen. (You may be prompted to install Chaos Tools, too. That can be retrieved at `http://drupal.org/project/ctools`).

Once they have been enabled, all of these modules should have checkmarks instead of empty check boxes.

Now that those are installed, let's look at the module administration for Looks. You will need to log in there (as the administrator for that site) and then go to **Administration | Modules**.

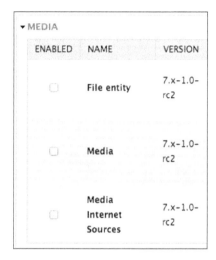

Notice that while the same modules are present on the page, *these modules have not been installed on the Looks site.*

So modules are shared in one sense: the same module files are available to every site in our multi-site. But, in another sense, they are not shared. Each site can enable or disable a module, and each site can have different configurations of a module.

Unshared modules

Sometimes you would like to have modules available on one site (or a few sites), but not to all. This may be for security reasons, simplicity, or performance.

Drupal allows you to accomplish this by storing modules in site configuration directories. Here we will walk though an example.

Let's say we want to install the **Field Text Formatter (textformatter)** module, which provides field formatters for text fields and taxonomy term fields. However, we only want this module to be on the Cooks site.

To do this, we will store the module in `sites/cooks.local/modules/contrib/`. This directory was not created automatically, so we will need to create it now. In a UNIX shell, this is done as follows:

```
$ cd sites/cooks.local
$ mkdir -p modules/contrib
```

Now we have our destination. As before, there are two ways we can install the package. We can manually download it from Drupal.org (`http://drupal.org/project/textformatter`) and then uncompress it in the `sites/cooks.local/modules/contrib/` directory. Or we can use Drush and have it do the work for us:

```
$ drush dl \
--destination=sites/cooks.local/modules/contrib \
textformatter
```

 Note that the command has been broken into three lines for the sake of formatting, but normally you will run it on a single line.

Most importantly, in order to get Drush to write the module into the Cooks site we need to add the `--destination` option, specifying the relative path to the `cooks.local` modules site.

Now if we log into the Cooks site as an administrator and go to **Administration | Modules**, we should see the **Field Text Formatter** module:

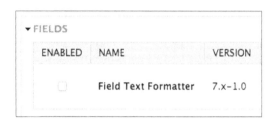

We can check the **Enabled** box and press the **Save Configuration** button as well. Now we have that module installed on `cooks.local`.

Now let's look at the Books site. Logging in on that site as the administrator, we can go to **Administration | Modules** and look for the **Field Text Formatter** module. But it will not be there. For when we install a module directly into a site's `modules` folder, it is not accessible to the other sites.

There is no standard way of sharing a module between some but not all sites. Typically, the safest way to make a module accessible to just some of the sites is to install it once in each site that will use it. This can make maintenance a little more difficult, but it will accomplish the task.

A note on using different versions of the same module

What do you do if one site requires a specific version of a module, while one of the other sites requires a different version of the same module?

Because of the way Drupal is constructed, you cannot install two versions of the same module in the `sites/all/modules/` directory. Attempting to do this will lead to fatal errors or, even worse, subtle bugs that arise from certain loading errors.

Likewise, it is not a good idea to install one version of a module in `sites/all/modules/` and another version of the module in `sites/SITENAME/modules/`. While Drupal itself will try to always load the site-specific version, there is no assurance that other modules will respect the same order of precedence that Drupal uses.

The best way of handling this situation is to install the modules in site-specific directories. So if Books were to require version 7.x-1.0 of some module while Looks required 7.x-1.1, the best way to proceed is this:

- Version 7.x-1.0 is installed in `sites/books.local/modules/contrib/`
- Version 7.x-1.1 is installed in `sites/looks.local/modules/contrib/`

This way, there is no chance that Drupal or any other module will confuse two different versions of the same module, as each site will have access only to its own version.

Modules and sharing (in summary)

We have walked through the various nuances of configuring modules in multi-site configurations. Before moving on to themes (which largely follow the same rules), here is a brief summary of the important points:

- Modules that are shared between all sites should go somewhere inside of `sites/all/modules/`.
- Modules that should be accessible to one site but not all should go inside of that site's `modules` directory, for example `sites/books.local/modules/`.
- When two sites require different versions of the same module, it is best to store the different versions inside of the site directories, and not store the module in `sites/all/modules/`, as that may cause errors or obscure bugs.
- And as a reminder, it is useful to separate modules inside of their respective module directories, into `contrib/` and `custom/` folders. This eases maintenance and readability.

Themes

In the section on modules, we saw how modules can be shared (to a certain extent) by placing them in `sites/all/modules/`, or how they can be installed for only a specific site by placing them in `sites/SITENAME/modules/`, where `SITENAME` is replaced by the site's name.

The same holds for themes. Multi-site themes can go in `sites/all/themes`, while site-specific themes can go in `sites/SITENAME/themes/`.

We can see this by first installing a theme into the `sites/all/themes/` directory. Let's begin with the **BlueMasters** theme. This is a stand-alone theme, which means it does not depend on a base theme. So we can install it in the usual ways. Either download it and uncompress it into `sites/all/themes`, or use Drush to do this for you:

```
$ drush dl bluemasters
```

Now when we log into Books as an administrator we can go to the **Appearance** page and see **Blue Masters** there. And if we go to the Cooks site, log in, and visit the **Appearance** settings, we will see the same thing:

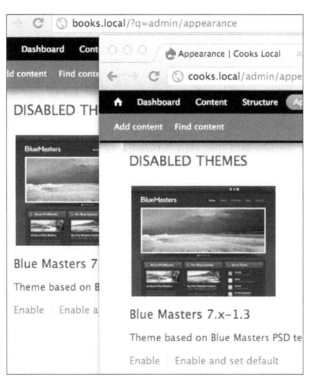

Now let's enable **BlueMasters** on Cooks. Click on **Enable and Set Default** to enable the theme and simultaneously set it as the site theme for our Cooks site. Now we can once again compare the Books and the Cooks theme pages:

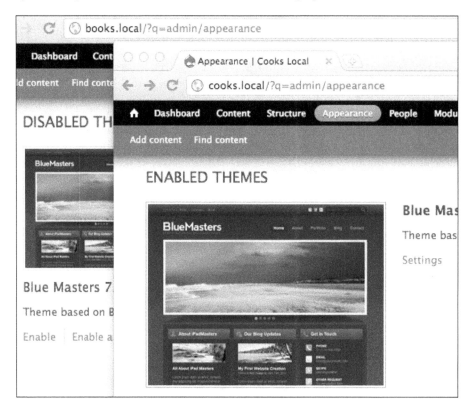

Notice how the Books site still lists **BlueMasters** as disabled, while the Cooks site has it enabled and set as default.

Just as with modules, when we talk about *sharing a theme between sites*, what we mean is that both sites have access to the theme. But while they share access to the theme's code and images, stylesheets and templates, they do not share configuration data.

 This can get tricky! Changing a template in a shared theme will change the template on all sites. But adding CSS or other styling through the administration interface typically will not result in sharing across sites.

The important detail that distinguishes when theme data is shared and when it is not is this:

- Anything that is stored in a code file (templates, CSS, info files, and so on) is shared
- Anything stored in the database (enabled status, settings, certain information about classes, or IDs) is site-specific

This can introduce some tedious nuances, as it is common practice to set some data through the administrative UI (storing it in the database) and then tweak CSS stylesheets to make use of that data. This strategy may not always work as desired on a multi-site setup, since the CSS files are shared across all three sites.

This is made slightly more complex by the addition of site-specific modules, which may have theme data accessible to one site, but not others. For modules can inject markup, styles, and JavaScript into the theme in a way that can significantly alter a site's appearance (and this is good). This can have tricky side-effects, though, when a theme is shared across sites, but modules are not.

This all sounds complex — it is — but there is a remedy: subthemes. We will start to move in that direction by looking at a few ready-made subthemes.

Subthemes and sharing

Since Drupal 6 it has been possible to base one theme on another theme. That is, we can start with a **base theme**, which defines major pieces of the site's layout and styling, but doesn't necessarily provide the final details. Then we can add a derivative theme (a subtheme) that begins with a base theme and fills in the details. It can even override things in the base theme that should be different.

The prevailing theory among Drupal theme developers is that when you are building your own theme, it is often best to begin with a base theme and build your own custom subtheme.

Now let's look at a practical example. The **AdaptiveTheme** (`http://drupal.org/project/adaptivetheme`) base theme has recently become fairly popular. It provides a base theme that supports a broad range of devices, including desktop and laptop computers, but also mobile devices like tablets and smart phones.

> **Which base theme?**
>
> Drupal.org has many base themes to choose from. **Zen**, the most popular, has received much acclaim from those who build custom themes. AdaptiveTheme is a relative newcomer, but has many ready-to-use subthemes. Tao, Omega, and Fusion Core are also popular. There are also base themes built on various grid layouts, such as the 960.gs system. If you are planning to build your own theme, take a look at the popular base themes and see which, if any, work best for you.

Let's install this base theme. We'll put it in the `sites/all/themes/` folder. Here's how to do it with Drush:

```
$ drush dl adaptivetheme
```

This actually installs three themes:

- **AT Core**: The base AdaptiveTheme theme
- **AT Subtheme**: A template project for building your own subtheme
- **AT Admin**: A fully functioning subtheme built on AT Core and intended to be used as an admin theme

When it comes to theming our user-facing site, none of these themes really provides us with what we want. This, for example, is what the site looks like with AT Core set as the theme:

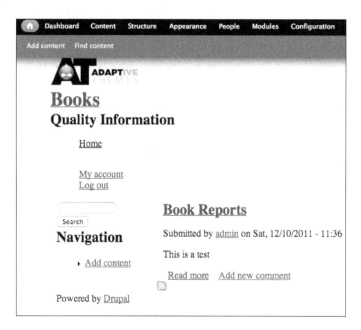

What is important about base themes, though, isn't what the base theme looks like, but what it provides for subthemes.

To see how this works, let's download a couple of subthemes. Here we are going to throw in a twist. We will install one subtheme on Cooks, and one on Looks.

Cooks will be using the **Corolla** subtheme (`http://drupal.org/project/corolla`) and Looks will be using **Pixture Reloaded** (`http://drupal.org/project/pixture_ reloaded`).

```
$ drush dl --destination=sites/cooks.local/themes corolla
$ drush dl --destination=sites/looks.local/themes pixture_reloaded
```

 If you do this by hand, you will need to create the themes directories for these two sites. Drush, on the other hand, will do it for you.

Next, I can go to each of my two sites—Cooks and Looks—and (as admin) go to the **Appearance** page and enable these themes as default.

Here is a screenshot of Looks running Pixture Reloaded, and Cooks running Corolla:

In this screenshot we can see how different the two themes are (even with no content). Yet both were built on the same base theme.

But there's something even more important going on here, the base theme was shared, but the subthemes are not. Since subthemes never actually alter the files in the base theme, this works very well. We can gain the advantage of having one shared theme at the core, but when it comes to tailoring each site to its audience, we split our subthemes.

Both Corolla and Pixture Reloaded are intended to be finished products. The assumption is that you won't need to dive into the code of these themes and start changing CSS or template files. In fact, if possible, you should avoid doing so.

However, there will be times when you will want to start with some theme (typically a base theme) and build your own style.

The best way to do this in a multi-site configuration (assuming you want to use the same base for more than one site) is to do as we did earlier, that is:

- Share a common base theme by putting it in `sites/all/themes`
- For each site's theme, put that theme in `sites/SITENAME/themes` (where `SITENAME` is the name of the particular site)

This strategy is good for minimizing the confusion between sites and their themes, and it gives you the freedom to modify a site's theme without worrying about unintended consequences to other sites.

You should now be at the point where you can install and manage themes on a multi-site Drupal instance. That takes us through the subject matter of the present chapter.

Summary

In this chapter we looked at how each site could be configured. We started out by looking at site settings, and saw how they are separate by default, but can be shared to a limited extent. Then we moved on to modules and themes. We saw that in a multi-site configuration, modules and themes can be shared, or they can be stored in just one site. We also saw how even shared modules can have different configurations on different sites. We looked at themes, focusing on the complications that arise between the tight coupling of a site's database data and its theme files. We looked at using site-specific subthemes, focusing on how that could mitigate the problem.

In the next chapter we are going to turn our attention to site administration. There, we will see once again how sharing code, but not database data, can introduce some subtle challenges.

4
Updating Multi-site Drupal

In previous chapters we have looked primarily at installation. In the first chapter, we prepared a system for installation. In the second chapter we installed Drupal and created three sites. And in the previous chapter we installed modules and themes. In this chapter, we are going to turn our attention to keeping Drupal up-to-date.

In this chapter, we will look at:

- Performing updates through the administrative web interface
- Updating Drupal's core in a multi-site configuration
- Updating modules and themes

While this is similar to the process used for a single site, there are some extra precautions and considerations. Performing updates in the proper order can prevent major multi-site outages.

Updating Drupal

There are two different "magnitudes" of upgrades. There are major upgrades and minor updates. A major upgrade updates Drupal from one major version (say, Drupal 6) to a newer one (Drupal 7). Because major Drupal versions indicate substantial changes, such upgrades are often time consuming, requiring many steps both before and after the actual installation of the software. We are not going to cover such upgrades.

Minor updates move from one point release to another newer point release. A **point release** is a software update that contains only bug fixes and minor feature changes. Its major version number remains the same, but its minor version (its point number) is incremented.

Drupal's current major version number is 7, and its minor version number (as of time of writing) is 12, so we have version 7.12.

Updating minor releases is much simpler than major upgrades, and should also be done regularly. Since most minor versions are released for security or stability reasons, they are typically quite important. In this section, we will look at updating Drupal multi-site configurations. The process differs from upgrading a single-site instance in that there are more steps, and the order of steps must be done carefully.

 Since a multi-site runs only one copy of Drupal, all of the sites on a multi-site install must be updated at the same time.

Multi-site updates differ from single-site updates in one crucial way: while Drupal's code needs to be updated only once, each individual site needs to go through the updating process. To keep site impact to a minimum (and to avoid catastrophes), doing these updates requires a special process.

Making backups

Anytime you are upgrading Drupal—single site or multi-site—you should make backup copies of everything.

Backing up Drupal is done in two stages. First, we must backup the files on the filesystem, and next we must backup the database.

Filesystem backups

We will use a UNIX-style shell to backup our files, but the same process can be done using a graphical front end to your filesystem.

Generally, it is best to backup the directory that contains Drupal, rather than just subdirectories inside of that directory. With a multi-site configuration, backing up the main Drupal directory will give us one large backup file containing the following:

- The main Drupal code
- Each of our sites/ directories
- The files stored in the files/ directory under each site

Given the setup we have walked through from *Chapter 1, Multi-site Drupal*, onwards, generating this backup is straightforward. Complex installations that use file sharing systems like NFS, Gluster, or network directories may handle the relationship between directories in complex ways. For example, the files directories may be mounted on different drives or even servers. In such situations the simple command here will not work for those. But unless you or your system administrator has done something like that, we can run a basic UNIX command to backup the entire directory.

> In a graphical file browser (such as Explorer on Windows or Finder on Mac) it is often possible to generate a compressed archive of a directory with a few mouse clicks. The following process, though, uses the command line. Either process will work.

Here I am using the Vagrant image discussed in the first few chapters. On a manually installed environment you may need to adjust the initial path.

```
$ cd /vagrant/public/drupal
$ tar -zcf drupal-backup.tgz www/
$ cp drupal-backup.tgz ~
```

In the first command, we simply change into the correct directory. We just want to backup the www/ directory in which we placed Drupal in *Chapter 2, Installing Drupal for Multi-site*.

Second, we run the `tar` command. This creates a single file called `drupal-backup.tgz` and then compresses all of the data from www/ into this file.

> The name TAR is short for Tape Archive. Originally, this program was intended for copying data onto a tape backup system. By default, TAR archives are not compressed. You use the -z flag to tell `tar` to zip the file, too.

The process of creating this file might take a few moments, and the resulting file may be surprisingly large. The simple site we have constructed is 5.5 MB on my filesystem. Production sites routinely grow to hundreds of megabytes.

The third command illustrates an important point: *Once you have created a backup file, move it somewhere safe.* The command just moves it to the user's home directory (represented by ~). That is a decent place. But leaving the file near Drupal is dangerous, as that is the place where we will be upgrading things. Accidentally overwriting or deleting our backup file could be disastrous.

Now we have our file system backup. Should you ever need to unpack it, you can use the `tar -zxf drupal_backup.tgz` command, that will extract the contents into a directory called www/.

Database backups

Backing up the files can be done all at once. But backing up the database is a little more complex.

We have three databases that need to be backed up, namely, `books_local`, `cooks_local`, and `looks_local`. While it is tempting to back all three up into the same file, that is typically not the best idea, for it leaves us in a situation in which we must either restore all three databases at once or manually break up the backup file into pieces. The former could cause data loss, and since database dump files may be hundreds of thousands of lines long the latter is impractical.

Since the databases are actually upgraded one at a time, it is more likely that only one will fail at a time. For that reason, it is better to simply make three backups, one for each database.

> The Drupal module called **Backup and Migrate** can ease and even automate the process of generating database backups. Learn more at http://drupal.org/project/backup_migrate.

We will be creating our backups on the command line, though most MySQL graphical front-ends can also do this.

> **Graphical Front-ends For MySQL**
> Popular Open Source MySQL front-ends include the web-based phpMyAdmin (which is installed but unconfigured in Vagrant) and the Mac OS X client Sequel Pro. Each of these has its own way of generating backups.

To generate a backup you will need to be able to connect to the MySQL database, and you will need to be able to authenticate as a user with permissions to run a full backup. Both your MySQL root user and your Drupal user should have sufficient permissions. Here we will use the root account:

```
$ mysqldump -h localhost -u root -p \
books_local > books_local_backup.mysql
```

The command has been broken into two lines for readability, but typically it is run on one line.

The command connects to a host (-h HOSTNAME) as user root (-u root), asks for a password prompt (-p), and then specifies the name of the database to dump (books_local). Using a shell redirect (>), we tell the shell to write the output of the command to the books_local_backup.mysql file.

As it stands, the resulting file will be an uncompressed plain text file full of SQL statements. Essentially, it is all of the SQL commands (in order) required to rebuild the database one statement at a time.

Should you ever need to restore the database, the typical way to do so is to issue a command like mysql –h localhost –u root -p < books_local_backup.mysql. This essentially does the reverse. It reads back in each line, executing it with the mysql program.

Repeat the dump for each database, storing the results in separate files:

```
$ mysqldump -h localhost -u root -p \
cooks_local > cooks_local_backup.mysql
$ mysqldump -h localhost -u root -p \
looks_local > looks_local_backup.mysql
```

Again, it is safest to place these files far away from the directory in which Drupal resides. We don't want to accidentally lose our backups.

With our data backed up, we are ready to run the next steps.

Putting Drupal in maintenance mode

Quite possibly the biggest disadvantage to a multi-site Drupal installation is that since all of the sites share the same code, anything that prevents the one copy of the code from operating will take all of the sites offline.

And this has steep implications when updating. *We need to put all of our sites into maintenance mode before we go any further.* And all of them ought to stay in maintenance mode until the very end of the upgrade process (though you can cut a few corners if you must).

For this reason, it is common to do multi-site maintenance at times that will not inconvenience your users, for even a minor update could take up to an hour. Most of the time, the most time-consuming aspect is generating the backups, and we have done that already. However, if anything goes wrong, all of the sites will be down until the issue is resolved.

With all of this in mind, the next step in our process is to log into Drupal as the administrator and go to **Administration | Configuration | Maintenance mode** and select the checkbox that says **Put site into maintenance mode**.

Make sure you press the **Save configuration** button after doing so.

 It is very important that you are logged in as the administrative account (user #1) to perform this step. Otherwise, permission issues could put your site into an uncertain state, locking out users and perhaps even generating fatal errors.

We must repeat this process for each of the Books, Cooks, and Looks sites. All of them need to be in maintenance mode before we proceed. Once a site is in maintenance mode, it is very important that you stay logged in on each site.

As long as you are logged in as an administrator and the site is in maintenance mode, you will see a notice like this:

Otherwise, the site will continue to look and act normally for you. But this is not what site visitors will see. Instead, they will see a page that looks like this (the exact theme the users see is something you can customize):

Site under maintenance

Cooks Local is currently under maintenance. We should be back shortly. Thank you for your patience.

Premium Drupal Themes

Once all three sites are in maintenance mode, we can move on to the next step.

Downloading and installing Drupal

The next step of the process is similar to a regular installation. We need to fetch the latest version of Drupal, and then we need to overwrite our current installation with the new files.

Fetching a new version

This process should be familiar to you already. You can use your web browser to go to Drupal.org and download the newest version, or you can use any number of tools to do this for you. For example, you can use Drush, if you have it installed. (It is already installed and configured in the Vagrant profile).

```
$ drush dl drupal
```

The command will download and unpack the latest stable version of Drupal into its own directory. In the examples, though, I will assume that Drupal has been downloaded through a web browser or a command-line tool like `wget`, and has not yet been unpacked.

Overwriting the existing files

The next step is to copy the new files into place. This can be dangerous, and if you have made any changes to files that came with Drupal, you will need to be very careful about what you do here.

 Two of the most commonly modified files in Drupal are `.htaccess` and `robots.txt`. Be very careful if you have made any changes to these, for if they are misconfigured, they can cause major problems with your site. A missing or broken `.htaccess` file can leave your site vulnerable to attacks, and a misconfigured `robots.txt` file can damage your search rankings with engines like Google and Bing.

There are a few different ways of copying a new version of Drupal.

The process that I've found to be the best blend of efficiency and accuracy is to put the updated version of Drupal in a new place, and then copy the files from one to the other, comparing as needed.

In the Vagrant profile, we store Drupal in `vagrant/public/drupal/www/`, so when we unpack the contents of the TAR archive, we will put them in the `vagrant/public/drupal` directory:

```
$ cd /vagrant/public/drupal
$ tar -zxvf drupal-7.12.tar.gz
```

Now we will have a new directory called `drupal-7.12`, which will contain the entire contents of Drupal. We can quickly see what changes were made by using the UNIX `diff` command:

```
$ diff -ru www drupal-7.12
```

The command compares the `drupal-7.12` directory with the www directory (which holds our existing site code.

The results of that command will look something like this (though probably a lot longer):

```
diff -ru www/modules/system/system.base.css drupal-7.12/modules/
system/system.base.css
--- www/modules/system/system.base.css    2011-11-30 20:59:37.000000000
-0800
+++ drupal-7.12/modules/system/system.base.css    2011-12-14
17:33:27.000000000 -0800
@@ -157,12 +157,9 @@
  .progress .percentage {
    float: right; /* LTR */
  }
-.progress-disabled {
-  float: left; /* LTR */
-}
 /* Throbber */
 .ajax-progress {
-  float: left; /* LTR */
+  display: inline-block;
 }
 .ajax-progress .throbber {
    background: transparent url(../../misc/throbber.gif) no-repeat 0px
-18px;
@@ -171,6 +168,9 @@
    margin: 2px;
    width: 15px;
 }
+.ajax-progress .message {
+  padding-left: 20px;
+}
 tr .ajax-progress .throbber {
    margin: 0 2px;
 }
```

The code is only a few lines from the real `diff`, which extends dozens of pages long. But this will give you a detailed list of every change between versions.

Lines that begin with a plus sign (+) are those that the new version will add, while lines that begin with a minus (-) will be removed.

If all looks good, we can copy all of the files at once. Or if you have made changes to your local copy of Drupal, you will need to comb through the `diff` and find out what you need to apply and what you don't.

Patch it!

The output generated by `diff` is in the format of a patch file. You can use the UNIX `patch` command to work with the output of `diff`. One workflow for patching is to save the output of `diff` to a file, hand edit the patches, and then apply the results with the `patch` command. A word of warning though, make sure your existing Drupal is backed up. A mistake in a patch can render your site useless.

For our purposes, we have made no changes to Drupal, so we can just copy the files over:

```
$ cp -a drupal-7.12/* www
```

Note that the command will NOT copy the `.gitignore` and the `.htaccess` files. To get those as well, execute this command:

```
$ cp -a drupal-7.12/.htaccess www
$ cp -a drupal-7.12/.gitignore www
```

Now we should have the most recent version of Drupal's code.

Checking the default.settings.php file

Finally, we should pay special attention to the file `sites/default/default. settings.php`. Recall that in *Chapter 2, Installing Drupal for Multi-site* we used `default.settings.php` as the template for each site's `settings.php` file. The default file contains useful information about the common settings that are supported, and what they do.

This file rarely changes, but when it does, it is typically because some major configuration parameter has been changed. A quick check of this file can help us catch any such changes. (You may find it easiest to use the `diff` program discussed earlier to run `diff www/sites/all/default/default.settings.php drupal-7.12/sites/all/default/default.settings.php`.)

If you see any major differences, such as a new parameter with documentation indicating that it is critical, you should follow the documentation provided therein and fix each of your sites' `settings.php` file. That said do not fret about moving minor changes (like changes in the wording of settings documentation). Since the default settings file is left in place, you can always refer back to it at a later time if necessary.

Running update.php

Often Drupal updates come with more than just code changes. They come with changes that need to be made in the database. So the next step is to run the update.php script.

You must be logged in as an administrator to run update.php. Earlier we put the site in maintenance mode, and I suggested there that we needed to stay logged in. So it should be unnecessary to try to log in again.

Now we can run the update tool on our Books site at the URL http://books.local/update.php.

Drupal database update

Use this utility to update your database whenev
is installed.

For more detailed information, see the upgradi
these terms mean you should probably contact

1. **Back up your database**. This process will
   case of emergency you may need to revert
2. **Back up your code**. Hint: when backing up
   in the 'modules' or 'sites/*/modules' direct
   auto-discovery mechanism.
3. Put your site into maintenance mode.
4. Install your new files in the appropriate loc

When you have performed the steps above, you

✓ Verify requirements
▶ **Overview**
Review updates
Run updates
Review log

Continue

Running the updater should bring us first to the overview page (the previous screenshot) which will suggest the same steps we have already taken. Once we press the **Continue** button, it will walk us through the update process.

If the Drupal updater requires updates, you should execute them. If there are no updates, the Drupal updater will display a message indicating this, and direct you back to the site. When the installer mentions "updates", what it means is database updates. Sometimes an update will add more information to the database, or remove unnecessary configuration data. Also, it may alter, add, or remove database tables (that is, it may make schema changes). Failure to apply all database updates may result in errors or even database corruption.

Since the updates are database updates, and since they alter only the databases of the site upon which `update.php` was run, it is absolutely imperative that `update.php` be run on each of your multi-sites.

In *Chapter 1, Multi-site Drupal* and *Chapter 2, Installing Drupal for Multi-site* I suggested that attempting to share database tables across multi-site instances can cause stability issues. Nowhere is this more prominent than when updating. Shared tables can become corrupted when updates change their data or structure. Occasionally, shared databases using prefixed tables can also be corrupted when add-on modules fail to honor prefixing rules. For these reasons, it is always preferable to store each site in its own database.

Furthermore, each Drupal instance can have different modules installed (and core comes with dozens of modules). If a module is not enabled on a site, it will not show up as needing an update. However, another site on the multi-site might use a module that needs an update. Therefore, just because one site update required no database updates does not mean that the other sites won't need a database update.

Once the updater has been run on each site we can take a look through the site, ensure that all is running well, and begin the last stage of the update.

Should an update fail, you may first wish to look online for information about your particular failure. You may also look to the Drupal community to help you solve the problem. In the worst case, you may have to restore your site by first restoring the backed-up files, and then restoring the database from your database dump file (see the *Database backups* section for the precise command to run).

If all went well, as it typically does, your sites are ready to be re-activated.

Taking the sites out of maintenance mode

Thus far we have made backups, updated the code, and run the database updater where necessary. We are now done, and should have a functional and up-to-date Drupal site. It is time to take the site off of maintenance mode.

Go back to **Administration | Configuration | Maintenance mode** and uncheck the box labeled **Put site into maintenance mode**. Press the **Save configuration** button to save this change and put your site back into regular mode.

This step must be repeated for every site (since every site is in maintenance mode).

Our sites are now all updated. And as we've seen while walking through the process, the important thing to keep in mind as we go is that we have one copy of the code and three different databases. Whenever we perform a task during updating, it's important that we determine whether it must be done once or three times. Keeping this distinction in mind will help answer that question.

Updating themes and modules

On any given Drupal site, at least several add-on modules and themes will be used. (I've seen sites with over 300 add-on modules.) It is important to keep those up to date, too.

On any of our sites, we can check at a glance whether or not there are newer modules available by going to **Administration | Reports | Available updates**.

The process for updating modules and themes is largely the same as performing a site update:

1. Put all of the sites in maintenance mode.
2. Download all of the modules and themes that you want to update.
3. Unpack them and put them into their appropriate locations. We have been placing our contributed modules in `sites/all/modules/contrib/` and our themes in `sites/all/themes/`.
4. Run `update.php` as we did before.
5. Bring all of the sites back out of maintenance mode.

This is the normal workflow for updating, and you can refer back to the *Updating Drupal* section for details.

Often the updates can be done from the command line, should you so desire, with Drush. To update the code for all of your modules and themes, you can run `drush updatecode`, and then for each site run `drush updatedb`. The only downside to using Drush for this task is that module owners do not always test with Drush, and (sometimes spurious) error messages may occur during a Drush update that would not otherwise arise during a browser-based update.

A minor complication

There is one minor complication to the previous process, that is it assumes that all of the modules and themes are shared between all of the sites. But what if the sites have their own modules? For example, what if the Cooks site has a recipes module that Looks and Books do not have? This module would reside in `sites/cooks.local/modules` instead of `sites/all/modules`.

This will require several modifications to the process:

- Instead of checking the **Available updates** report for just one site, you will need to check all three.

- When downloading modules and themes, you will need to make sure to put each module and theme in the right directory. This will include your `sites/SITENAME/modules` and `sites/SITENAME/themes` directories.

- Finally, make sure to run `update.php` on each site, for we cannot infer from one site that there are no updates on the other sites if sites have their own modules and themes.

Keeping a multi-site Drupal instance up to date is a little more challenging than maintaining just a single site (though it is still easier than maintaining multiple single sites). With a little diligence, though, the process can be managed.

Summary

In this chapter we have focused on the process of keeping our sites up to date. We first looked at updating Drupal's core, and then we turned our attention to updating modules and themes.

The important aspect of updating a multi-site is to make sure we prevent an update on one site from causing errors on the other sites. For that reason, we were careful to put sites in maintenance mode before updating code and running the database updater.

In the next chapter we will look at some advanced configuration options for multi-site Drupal installations.

5
Advanced Multi-sites

In the previous chapters we have seen how to install, configure, and update multi-site Drupal. In this chapter we are going to look at various strategies for accomplishing advanced configurations.

Rather than explaining the details of a module or two, this chapter addresses specific topics with general explanations and module suggestions. Each module discussed here comes with its own documentation on how it is used.

These are the feature categories that we will look at in this chapter:

- Handling favicons and robots
- Sharing authentication across sites
- Sharing content across sites
- Sharing structural elements across sites
- Cross-site search

Favicons and robots

There are certain files that various web agents expect to find at predefined URLs on your server. Drupal provides some of these files at fixed locations within the Drupal distribution. That is, these files are actual files stored on the filesystem, not paths whose content Drupal generates. This can cause issues when working with multi-site Drupal instances, since often each site needs its own copy of these files. In this section we will look at modules that solve this problem for two specific types of file, namely, favicons and robots files.

Favicons ("Favorite Icons"), the little images that show up on browser tabs and in bookmarks, are one example. Some web agents assume these files will be accessible at your site's root with the name `favicon.ico`, for example `http://example.com/favicon.ico`.

> Drupal allows you to specify a favicon in a theme's settings, but it relies on the user agent to find out where the favicon is located (by reading part of an HTML document). It does not create a file at the path `/favicon.ico`.

In a multi-site configuration, we want Drupal to provide a different favicon for each site. And we want this file to be served at the expected URL. This is best accomplished by using the **Favicon** module (http://drupal.org/project/favicon). It will allow each site to declare its own favicon, and each site will handle requests for the favicon at the canonical `/favicon.ico` URL.

Some web agents—notably search engine crawlers—look for a file called `robots.txt`. Search crawlers expect to find information in this file that tells them what parts of the site should be indexed. The contents of this file can figure prominently in search engine optimization, and a well-configured robots file can substantially improve a site's appearance in search engine results on the likes of Google and Bing.

By default, Drupal only supports a single `robots.txt` file that is served out for all of the sites in a multi-site. But many multi-site configurations need something more complex. URL patterns are likely to be different from site to site, and a one-size-fits-all robots file is untenable. Each site may need to provide its own robots file.

For this reason, there is a contributed module called **RobotsTxt** (http://drupal.org/project/robotstxt) that provides an administrative interface on each site, which you can use to set site-specific robots directives.

> **Use this on single-site installations, too!**
>
> Since Drupal core comes with a `robots.txt` file, it will try to overwrite this file each time you perform an upgrade. To avoid a search crawler catastrophe, you may find it better to install the RobotsTxt module and store your robot configuration in the database.

Similar Drupal modules exist for dealing with features that web agents expect to find at specific paths. The **sitemap** module (http://drupal.org/project/xmlsitemap) is another example. It allows each site to have a specific set of rules to generate the robust sitemap files that Google, Bing, and other search engines use to discover the content on your site.

Shared authentication

One often-desired feature on multi-site installations is to share user accounts across sites. The term "user accounts" is ambiguous, though. Do we want Single Sign On (SSO), where the same username and password work in various sites, or do we want something more—like having entire user profiles synchronized across our multi-sites?

Often, loosely affiliated sites will share authentication credentials, allowing one to use the same credentials to log in on multiple sites, yet each site will have its own user-specific profile where the user can, for example, set a profile picture or write a biography. This method is sometimes called Single (or Shared) Sign On (SSO).

Sites with a stronger affiliation may require a greater degree of integration. A user may have a single robust user profile available to all of the sites on this tightly knit network. But this requires more work than simply validating credentials for login.

It is not the case that one of these is better than the other. The requirements of any given set of sites will determine which of these two methods is most appropriate.

Here is a brief survey of several different approaches to sharing authentication credentials across multiple sites. Most of these solutions were designed to work beyond multi-site configurations. To that end, they can be used to authenticate between different servers. But all of them should also work with a multi-site as discussed in this book.

Before providing an overview of several methods, I will give one word of warning: *There is no simple solution*. Each method documented here requires significant work, the details of which are beyond the scope of this book.

OpenID and other authentication services

First, let's begin with the least sophisticated. Drupal comes with a module called **OpenID**. This allows users to use a specific shared ID (an Open ID) and use it on many different sites. OpenID shares the least amount of information between sites. Only the OpenID identifier (usually a URL) is shared. Users can even have different usernames on different sites.

Google, Facebook, and others have expressed support for this model, and obtaining an OpenID is easy. In this model, when a user supplies a login ID, the Drupal site interacts with a remote OpenID server. The user is prompted to authenticate to the OpenID server (not the Drupal server), and that server then informs Drupal when the user successfully authenticates.

If you use an external OpenID provider, you can enable and use the OpenID module. This will allow your users to sign into each multisite with the same OpenID account, though each site will actually have its own user account record. This same OpenID account can be used not only on your sites, but on other Internet sites that support OpenID authentication. For this reason it is considered "open", as it is not limited to only a few sites.

OpenID isn't the only solution for authentication services. Similar configurations can be achieved using Twitter, Google, Facebook, and other backends. You can search the Drupal.org module listing for modules that provide integration with your service of choice.

LDAP and Directory services

Another alternative is to use a local directory server or authentication service like LDAP, ActiveDirectory, CAS, or Kerberos. Under this setup, accounts are maintained on a separate server, and Drupal communicates with these servers to verify credentials.

Unlike OpenID, though, these servers know more about the user, and can share this information with Drupal and other servers. In other words, they are often used for much more than simple authentication. This method can be very powerful for large internal networks (like corporations and educational institutions), but is probably overly complex for a simple multi-site.

One advantage to this solution is that accounts can be handled independently. Dedicated servers with strictly enforced access control policies are desirable if security is an important goal. Another advantage is that support for LDAP, Active Directory (which is a flavor of LDAP), CAS, and Kerberos enjoy widespread support. From operating systems to servers to client programs, many tools can perform authentication and authorization using these services.

But the disadvantage is that maintaining directory or authentication servers adds another layer of complexity to your configuration. Often, managing directory and authentication services is as complex (if not more complex) than managing a web server application stack.

LDAP support is provided in the LDAP module (`http://drupal.org/project/ldap`) and related modules, while Kerberos support is found in the Kerberos Authentication module (`http://drupal.org/project/kerberos_authentication`). **CAS (Central Authentication Service)** can be found at `http://drupal.org/project/cas`.

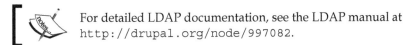 For detailed LDAP documentation, see the LDAP manual at
`http://drupal.org/node/997082`.

Using the Services module

The **Services** module (`http://drupal.org/project/services`) provides an underlying framework for sharing Drupal data with other sites. It provides a sophisticated mechanism for authenticating remote clients and granting those clients programmatic access to Drupal information. Using **Representational State Transfer (REST)**, provides an HTTP-based **API (Application Programming Interface)** to which other network programs can connect.

In short, it makes it possible for other programs (including other Drupal instances) to connect to Drupal and access data.

And with the help of the **Services SSO Client** (`http://drupal.org/project/services_sso_client`) and **Services SSO Server Helper** (`http://drupal.org/project/services_sso_server_helper`) modules, it can be used for shared authentication.

This is a promising approach, though configuring the Services module can be tedious and time consuming, as it requires detailed knowledge of Drupal's internal data structures and (on many occasions) code. The SSO Client and Server Helper modules are under active development at the time of this writing, but as they stabilize this may become the best way to share sign-in data between sites on a general multi-site configuration.

Using Bakery for SSO

Drupal.org shares authentication information across `http://drupal.org`, `http://groups.drupal.org`, and other sites. How does it accomplish this? Several members of the core infrastructure team built and manage a module called **Bakery** (`http://drupal.org/project/bakery`). This module can share authentication information between multiple sites, provided all of the sites are under the same second-level domain. That is, you can share authentication between `http://www.example.com` and `http://dev.example.com`, but you couldn't share authentication between `http://www.example.com` and `http://www.anotherexample.com`.

Why this limitation? Because Bakery relies heavily on browser cookies for storing shared tokens, yet by design cookies can only be shared with sites underneath a given top domain.

The domain restriction is the biggest limitation of Bakery. But given the deep commitment of the Drupal community, Bakery is well-maintained and stable.

Sharing a user database

The last method of shared authentication is sharing database tables between all of the instances. The strategy here is to have a single database (or copy of the user tables) that is shared among all of the multi-site instances.

While this method has been around for years, it remains fraught with difficulties. Upgrading is tremendously complex, and there are security issues with sharing such data in this way. A couple of modules were created to streamline this functionality, but the latest of these, SSO (`http://drupal.org/project/sso`) is no longer maintained.

If you are interested in attempting to share database tables, the best place to start is in the **Advanced and multisite installation** section of the complete **Installation Guide**, which has a section entitled **Share tables across instances (not recommended)** (`http://drupal.org/node/22267`). However, this method ought to be considered a last resort.

Shared content

Shared authentication is a popular but tricky problem to solve. Another often-requested feature for multi-site installations is sharing content.

The multi-site design was not initially intended to share content. In fact, it was intended to *not* share content. Be that as it may, there are a few ways of accomplishing this.

As with shared authentication, one possibility is to attempt to share database tables between different sites on a multi-site. On occasion, users report having attempted this method on their own sites. But this method is also fraught with difficulties. Security is difficult, updates require special care, and there is constant danger of what is called a "race condition", where two different sites vie for control of the same resource. Consequently, this method should be avoided.

There are a few other more reliable methods, though.

Sharing content with Services and Deploy

The **Services** module (`http://drupal.org/project/services`) discussed in the previous section provides all of the architecture required for sharing content. However, it doesn't provide an easy-to-use interface for sharing. But the **Deploy** module (`http://drupal.org/project/deploy`), which is built on Services, can be used to move content from one server to another.

Deploy is a good fit if you want to synchronize content from one site to another. The canonical case for Deploy is running a staging server (where content is authored) and a live server (where users come to view the content), and deploying content from the staging server onto the live server as it is ready.

Since Deploy is workflow-based, it requires substantial effort to configure and maintain. The Drupal 7 release has not yet stabilized, so investing in Deploy will require experience in PHP coding.

Domain Access as a multi-site alternative

If sharing content is a high priority, the best solution is to move away from the core multi-site configuration discussed in this book. Built as a more sophisticated method of hosting multiple domains on a single Drupal instance, **Domain Access** (`http://drupal.org/project/domain`) uses only one database. Instead of creating separate Drupal installations (one for each site) Domain Access creates a single Drupal instance that can listen on multiple hostnames, reacting differently depending on which hostname the client requests.

Sites can look entirely different, having unique navigation, themes, and content. But content can also be shared. In addition, there is only one administration interface for all of the sites. This is great in cases where one person or group must manage all of the sites, but if various sites are managed by different administrators, it can be tricky (and sometimes impossible) to grant the right level of permissions to the different administrators.

Because it is stable, continually maintained, and widely used, the Domain Access module is the best choice if content sharing is a requirement for your multi-site configuration. But be aware that it is complicated and requires detailed knowledge of Drupal concepts and components.

The Virtual Site module

Finally, another promising (but currently incomplete) module will provide a different way to run a single site and configure it to act as different sites under different conditions. The **Virtual Site** module (`http://drupal.org/project/virtual_site`), which was developed for Drupal 6 and is currently being updated, promises just this.

By adjusting which configuration parameters it uses based on the nature of the request (what domain, what browser type, and so on), the Virtual Site module can use different configuration parameters. For example, it can support different themes, different site names, and different menus.

 Virtual Site and Domain Access have substantial feature overlap. While Domain Access is clearly more stable and more frequently used, the Virtual Site module does have some interesting features, such as the robust support for declaring conditions.

Unlike Drupal's built-in multi-site capability, Virtual Site can switch on conditions other than domain name. For example, it can be configured to serve a different "site" to mobile browsers than to desktop browsers.

But Virtual Site shares one database (and one set of nodes, comments, users, and so on) for all of the virtual sites it hosts. In this way it is on the opposite end of the spectrum from the built-in multi-site, which uses separate databases for each site.

Currently, Virtual Site for Drupal 7 is still under active development. It is not ready for production use. Hopefully, though, it will soon stabilize and be a viable solution for multi-site developers.

Shared structure

Sometimes multi-sites do not need to share content, but would benefit from sharing content types, permissions, views, contexts, formats, and other structural data. Typically, this data is stored in the database, and since Drupal multi-sites typically do not share the same database tables, they cannot automatically share this data.

However, the **Features** module (`http://drupal.org/project/features`) provides this capability. Features is a tool that transforms certain Drupal structures into versioned modules.

Features is by no means specific to multi-site configurations. Most commonly, it is used to share features between completely unrelated sites.

Let's imagine a practical scenario. Imagine that we have created a blog. On one of the sites in our multi-site we have defined the content type, the permissions, and the views necessary for this blog. But now we want to use this exact blog structure on all of the sites on the multi-site. This is what Features allows us to do. We can create a new Feature (a process done through the administrative interface) on our first site, assigning content types, permissions, views, and even blocks to this feature.

Once the Feature is completely built, we can export it, which generates a module containing all of the code necessary for replicating the exact same structure on another site. By putting this module in our `sites/all/modules` folder we can make it available to all of the sites on our multi-site setup. To turn the feature on for one of the other sites, we can simply go to the **Modules** screen in Drupal's administration. The module will appear in the list of available modules, and all we need to do is enable it.

Features is a great tool for sharing Drupal structure across sites. While it is relatively stable on Drupal 7, it is still in its beta stages. Even so, it provides a fantastic toolset for sharing across sites.

While Features is not designed to share content, there are various projects that will likely extend Features' capabilities to do this. In the future, Features may be a good candidate for limited sharing of content between sites.

Searching across sites

The last topic to cover in this chapter is site search. The core Drupal server comes with a built-in search engine. This engine can index all of the content on a site, allowing visitors to search for content.

Because it stores all of its information in the database, each Drupal site in a multi-site setup can have its own search engine.

But what if we want to provide a single search instance that can search content across all of our sites? In this case, when a user searches on our fabled `books.local` site, that user would see `looks.local` and `cooks.local` content as well.

This particular form of cross-site searching cannot be done with the built-in search engine. However, since Drupal's search is pluggable, we can use an add-on module to provide this service.

The most popular search engine alternative for Drupal 7 is the **Apache Solr** module (`http://drupal.org/project/apachesolr`). This module relies on an external Apache Solr server (`http://lucene.apache.org/solr/`) to handle the technical details of searching.

Because it requires an external server (which you will need to set up and manage), Solr is harder to maintain than the built-in Drupal search. But it integrates well with multi-site Drupal. Each site in a multi-site can be configured to use the same Solr instance, and that one Solr instance can search data for all of your sites.

Hosted Solr

Acquia (`http://acquia.com`) provides a hosted Solr service for Drupal sites. Once you have signed up for their search services, you can configure your multi-sites to store content on their Solr servers. This alleviates the burden of running your own copy of Solr.

In addition to the Drupal Apache Solr module, there are several other search alternatives, such as the **Xapian** module (`http://drupal.org/project/xapian`), that can be used to access external search services.

When it comes to running a search service within Drupal, and not relying upon an external server, options are limited. The new **Zend Lucene** project (`http://drupal.org/project/zend_lucene`) may at some point provide multi-site search capabilities, but at this time of writing it does not.

Summary

The purpose of this short chapter has been to point beyond a simple multi-site configuration to various modules that can extend multi-site capabilities. We briefly looked at authentication, shared content, shared structure, and cross-site searching.

Drupal's multi-site capabilities can make it easier to host many websites. As we've seen throughout the book, there are challenges to setting up multi-site, but the benefits outweigh those challenges.

Finally, we have diligently focused on the multi-site capabilities built into Drupal. But as I said at the beginning, multi-site is only one way of hosting multiple Drupal sites. Wisely choosing the best strategy for your needs will make both immediate set up and long-term maintenance easier. Multi-site may indeed be the best fit for your own needs, but if not, take a look at some of the other options Drupal provides, from simply hosting multiple instances of Drupal separately to using Domain Access for deep sharing of content. Thousands upon thousands of websites rely upon Drupal. And this is largely due to Drupal's tremendous flexibility.

Index

H

hosts file
  about 18
  using 19
HTTP protocol 9
HTTPS 9

I

IIS 21
installing
  Drupal 65
  subthemes 55, 56
  tailored Vagrant project 14, 15
  themes 53, 54
  unshared modules 50, 51
INSTALL.txt document 42
Internet Service Provider (ISP) 13
IP address 18

K

Kerberos 76

L

LAMP 14
LDAP 76
LDAP module 76
Lighttpd 21
Linux 10
Linux Apache MySQL PHP. *See* **LAMP**

M

maintenance mode
  Drupal, placing in 63-65
Media Internet Sources module 49
Media module 48, 49
modules
  and sharing 52
  configuring 47
  sharing 48-50
  updating 71
multi-site
  and Drupal 10-12

multi-site configuration
  selecting 12, 13
  versus standard single-site configurations
    6, 7
multi-site Content Management System 6
multi-site Drupal
  major upgrade 59
  minor updates 59, 60
  updating 59, 60
multi-site hosting 6
MySQL
  about 10
  configuring 24
  graphical front-end 62

N

new virtual machine
  connecting to 16, 17
Nginx 21

O

online Drupal installation manual
  URL 42
OpenID 75

P

patch command 68
PHP 10
Pixture Reloaded 57
point release 59

Q

quality assurance (QA) 9

R

README.txt document 42
Representational State Transfer (REST) 77
robots
  about 74
  handling 74
RobotsTxt module 74

VirtualBox
  about 10, 14
  URL 14
virtual hosting
  about 21
  using, for each domain 23
virtual server 13
Virtual Site module 80

W

Web 16
web installer 37, 38

web servers
  about 21
  Apache 21
wget command 29

X

Xapian module 82

Z

Zen 56
Zend Lucene project 82

Thank you for buying
Drupal 7 Multi-sites Configuration

About Packt Publishing

Packt, pronounced 'packed', published its first book "*Mastering phpMyAdmin for Effective MySQL Management*" in April 2004 and subsequently continued to specialize in publishing highly focused books on specific technologies and solutions.

Our books and publications share the experiences of your fellow IT professionals in adapting and customizing today's systems, applications, and frameworks. Our solution based books give you the knowledge and power to customize the software and technologies you're using to get the job done. Packt books are more specific and less general than the IT books you have seen in the past. Our unique business model allows us to bring you more focused information, giving you more of what you need to know, and less of what you don't.

Packt is a modern, yet unique publishing company, which focuses on producing quality, cutting-edge books for communities of developers, administrators, and newbies alike. For more information, please visit our website: www.packtpub.com.

About Packt Open Source

In 2010, Packt launched two new brands, Packt Open Source and Packt Enterprise, in order to continue its focus on specialization. This book is part of the Packt Open Source brand, home to books published on software built around Open Source licences, and offering information to anybody from advanced developers to budding web designers. The Open Source brand also runs Packt's Open Source Royalty Scheme, by which Packt gives a royalty to each Open Source project about whose software a book is sold.

Writing for Packt

We welcome all inquiries from people who are interested in authoring. Book proposals should be sent to author@packtpub.com. If your book idea is still at an early stage and you would like to discuss it first before writing a formal book proposal, contact us; one of our commissioning editors will get in touch with you.

We're not just looking for published authors; if you have strong technical skills but no writing experience, our experienced editors can help you develop a writing career, or simply get some additional reward for your expertise.

Drupal 7

ISBN: 978-1-84951-286-2   Paperback: 416 pages

Create and operate any type of website quickly and efficiently

1. Set up, configure, and deploy a Drupal 7 website

2. Easily add exciting and powerful features

3. Design and implement your website's look and feel

4. Promote, manage, and maintain your live website

5. Extended media coverage

Drupal 7 Development by Example Beginner's Guide

ISBN: 978-1-84951-680-8   Paperback: 270 pages

Follow the creation of a Drupal website to learn, by example, the key concepts of Drupal 7 development and HTML5

1. A hands-on, example-driven guide to programming Drupal websites

2. Discover a number of new features for Drupal 7 through practical and interesting examples while building a fully functional recipe sharing website

3. Learn about web content management, multi-media integration, and e-commerce in Drupal 7

Please check **www.PacktPub.com** for information on our titles

Drupal 7 Business Solutions

ISBN: 978-1-84951-664-8   Paperback: 378 pages

Build powerful website features for your business

1. Build a Drupal 7 powered website for your business rapidly

2. Add blogs, news, e-commerce, image galleries, maps, surveys, polls, and forums to your website to beat competition

3. Complete example of a real world site with clear explanation

Drupal 7 Themes

ISBN: 978-1-84951-276-3   Paperback: 320 pages

Create new themes for your Drupal 7 site with a clean layout and powerful CSS styling

1. Learn to create new Drupal 7 themes

2. No experience of Drupal theming required

3. Discover techniques and tools for creating and modifying themes

4. The first book to guide you through the new elements and themes available in Drupal 7

Please check **www.PacktPub.com** for information on our titles

www.ingramcontent.com/pod-product-compliance
Lightning Source LLC
Chambersburg PA
CBHW082111070326
40689CB00052B/4496